Reynolds Price

Twayne's United States Authors Series

Warren French, Editor

Indiana University, Indianapolis

TUSAS 450

REYNOLDS PRICE
(1933–   )

Photograph by Stathis Orphanos

Reynolds Price

By Constance Rooke

University of Victoria

Twayne Publishers • *Boston*

Reynolds Price

Constance Rooke

Copyright © 1983 by G. K. Hall & Company
All Rights Reserved
Published by Twayne Publishers
A Division of G. K. Hall & Company
70 Lincoln Street
Boston, Massachusetts 02111

Book Production by Marne B. Sultz

Book Design by Barbara Anderson

Printed on permanent/durable acid-free
paper and bound in the United States of
America.

Library of Congress Cataloging in Publication Data

Rooke, Constance, 1942–
    Reynolds Price.

    (Twayne's United States authors series ; TUSAS 450)
    Bibliography: p. 151
    Includes index.
    1. Price, Reynolds, 1933–   —Criticism and
interpretation.   I. Title.   II. Series.
PS3566.R54Z86   1983   813'.54   83–12720
ISBN 0-8057-7390-8

Contents

About the Author

Constance Rooke was born in New York City in 1942. She received her B.A. from Smith College in 1964, an M.A. from Tulane University in 1966, and a Ph.D. from the University of North Carolina at Chapel Hill in 1973. Her dissertation was on Wright Morris. Since 1969 she has taught in the English Department at the University of Victoria in British Columbia, Canada, where she is currently an associate professor. She is the editor of the *Malahat Review*.

Her critical essays have appeared in a wide variety of American and Canadian journals (*Studies in Short Fiction, Canadian Literature,* etc.) and have treated writers as various as Keats, Camus, George Eliot, Edith Wharton, Emily Dickinson, Saul Bellow, Katherine Anne Porter, Robert Frost, Stephen Crane, Margaret Laurence, and P. K. Page. She has also published numerous short stories in magazines such as the *Southern Review,* as well as book reviews and interviews with contemporary writers. Several stories were written in collaboration with her husband, Leon Rooke.

Preface

Reynolds Price is generally regarded as among the most important Southern novelists of his generation. Although his fiction often and with considerable brilliance employs Southern settings and themes which we have come to expect from Southern fiction, his work is not essentially about the South. This study attempts to convey how strongly individual, even idiosyncratic his fiction is, how relentlessly it proceeds from a single, complex vision of the world. Although Price deals with nearly all of the largest human questions, so that it would be a mistake to describe him as a narrow writer, his work has an intensely personal, almost obsessive quality. His vision is both more consistent and darker than many of his readers have supposed.

The biographical section of the first chapter attempts to clothe the bare facts of the author's life with an interpretation of those facts given by Price. This has seemed necessary because of the very considerable extent to which Price's fiction draws upon his life, particularly upon his early experiences. The introductory chapter also attempts briefly to place the author in a Southern context and to define some of his attitudes to writing and to other writers. Price's work as a poet, essayist, and translator is treated summarily, with an emphasis upon the homogeneity of the author's vision which is argued throughout the chapter and indeed the book. The introduction also supplies a brief discussion of the author's style, a subject which reappears in the treatment of individual works, and a description of the author's central thematic concerns.

Chapters two through eight treat Price's books of fiction in the order of their publication. The organization varies from one chapter to the next, according to the special requirements of the work under consideration. The dominant method is explication, mainly because the difficulty of Price's fiction suggests that this would be most welcome to the reader. Imagery, links between the books, and the relationship of each work to Price's central theme are given special emphasis.

My thanks are due to Reynolds Price, who has been unfailingly gracious and helpful in all of my contacts with him, and above all to Terence Young, to whom I am deeply indebted for research assistance and illuminating dialogue throughout the preparation of this book.

Constance Rooke

University of Victoria

Chronology

Chapter One
Christian Solitary
Biography

Reynolds Price was born during the deep Depression, on February 1, 1933, in Warren County, North Carolina, at his mother's family home in Macon. The delivery was hard, and Price has never forgotten that he "nearly killed . . . did indeed maim"[1] his mother, or that his father swore to God he would give up drink if mother and child survived. The times also were hard. His father, for instance, lost their home because he could not borrow fifty dollars. The Depression, Price says, "shaped and confirmed [his] earliest fears, demanded the building of [his] earliest defenses against the anonymous forces of ruin, humiliation before one's kin."[2] His fantasies as a child were those of Dickensian orphans; his terrors were "destitution and abandonment."[3] Sometimes he imagined himself the "child of unknown parents, merely adopted by the Prices whose lives [he] now greatly complicated."[4]

Will Price worked as an appliance salesman. In a brief elegy composed some ten years after his father's death, Reynolds Price describes his discovery of a demonstration record made by Will. He listens again to his father's sales pitch, "his endless bottled plea for hope,"[5] and recoils at his memory of all his father was obliged to endure. Thinking particularly of his father's long battle against drink, his years of unrewarding labor, and his painful death, Reynolds invites a youthful portrait of his father to "cancel all plan of me, let me not be."[6] Thus he assumes responsibility for the harnessed, fatal course of his father's life, precisely as he had taken the blame for nearly killing his mother. The fear of betrayal by loved ones or by vast external forces (such as were imaged by the Depression) was accompanied by a sense of guilt—all this despite the love that his parents gave abundantly, and he returned.

In many ways it was a happy childhood. There was too much moving about, from one North Carolina town to another; and there was loneliness, for Reynolds was an only child until the age of eight and had few playmates. But consolation and excitement were supplied by a close relationship with his parents and by the presence of aunts, uncles, and cousins. There were also books, provided especially for Reynolds. His was a family of gifted talkers, however, rather than a bookish one—and Reynolds was an avid, very retentive listener. Preferring the company of adults, "shooed away" only when the jokes became bawdy, he had ample time to relish how a story would be repeated in "exactly the same words and with a kind of delight of discovery as though it had never been told before." The talkative quality of Price's fiction, the shapeliness of his dialogue, the insistence upon certain favored words, and the obsession with family history obviously owe much to this early experience.

Although Price did some writing in childhood and adolescence, mainly poetry and a few plays, he supposed then that he would become a painter. Again, the sharply pictorial quality of his fiction may be seen as deriving from that early and continuing interest. Whatever works he attempted, however—"writing, drawing, painting, being local boy-soprano"—were understood even at the time as "efforts to achieve dignity."[7] Price did these things because he was more or less good at them, whereas he was "absolutely hopeless in sports,"[8] and because he wished to assert his own worth in the face of extreme unpopularity, a "miserable adolescence . . . [which was] the seed for a great deal that has come afterward."[9] Before he left high school, Price had settled on writing as his chief skill and salvation.

In 1951 Price entered a new world at Duke University and began to experience the friendships that would play an important role in his adult life. In his freshman year Price began the story that would become "Michael Egerton," which he completed in his senior year and showed to Eudora Welty when she came to Duke to deliver her celebrated talk on "Place in Fiction." Her encouragement and the criticism Price received from professors such as William Blackburn were enormously helpful to the young writer, but Price devoted little of his time during these undergraduate years to the writing of fiction. Instead, he prepared for that career by reading and studying voraciously. His labors were rewarded by a Rhodes Scholarship. From 1955 to 1958, Price studied at Merton College, Oxford University, under Helen Gardner and Lord David Cecil; he wrote a thesis on Milton's *Samson Agonistes*, as well as several of the stories that would be collected in *The Names and Faces of Heroes*, and made notes for his first novel.

Price then returned to Duke University where with brief intermissions he has been teaching ever since. He had determined to be a writer who taught, an ambition which Duke has gladly fostered by requiring that Price teach only one semester each year—usually Milton and a class in the writing of narrative prose. When he returned to Duke in 1958, Price began work on the novel he had planned while at Oxford. He finished *A Long and Happy Life* in 1961; and it appeared the next year in its entirety in *Harper's Magazine*—a very considerable honor for an unknown writer. It also initiated his association with the Atheneum press that continues to the present. Critical response was almost unanimously enthusiastic.

In 1961 Price returned to England to complete work on *The Names and Faces of Heroes*, which was published in 1963 and was very favorably received. He next began the novel that would become *The Surface of Earth*, but abandoned that for *A Generous Man*, published in 1966. Again the reviews were gratifying. With *Love and Work*, published in 1968, Price experienced for the first time a seriously divided critical response. Many of his readers were dismayed by its gloom and by the shift away from naive, rural adolescents to a protagonist vastly more sophisticated, a writer-teacher whom they could not avoid thinking was somehow and unfortunately Price himself. This new direction was confirmed by *Permanent Errors*, a short story collection published in 1970 which took several of its literary, intellectual protagonists out of North Carolina altogether. Both *Love and Work* and *Permanent Errors* had their fervent supporters, however, and the latter book met with a good deal of intelligent appreciation.

In 1972 Price published a distinguished, miscellaneous collection called *Things Themselves*, which included commentaries on his own work as well as that of other writers, a version of his thesis on *Samson Agonistes*, and scenes from a screenplay of *A Long and Happy Life*. During this period he was again at work on *The Surface of Earth*, which was published in 1975. The reviews of that lengthy, ambitious novel were again mixed, and many readers seemed unsure of their response. A family chronicle of great and peculiar intensity, *The Surface of Earth* was not the sort of book its reviewers were accustomed to finding on their desks. In 1977 Price published *Early Dark*, a play based on *A Long and Happy Life*; and in 1978 *A Palpable God* appeared, contemporary biblical translations which met with a warm reception from scholars and other readers. *The Source of Light* came out in 1981; a sequel to *The Surface of Earth*, it had mixed reviews.

Reynolds Price has never married. He lives alone in a rather large and beautiful house near Durham. Its setting is rural, and the interior contains those fine artifacts, drawings, and paintings which he began

to collect while at Oxford. Price departs from this stationary life occasionally, to lecture elsewhere or for vacations; but he rarely stays
away long, because he is a rooted person who can work only where
he is "surrounded by familiar and unthreatening things."[10] People
are his "household gods," as illustrated by the photographs of friends
and family that fill his home, which he says are there for the sake of
his work, of which their originals are both "cause" and "audience."[11]
But often the only living person in his house is Reynolds Price, for
his work gets done in solitude.

Attitudes to Writing

Price obviously writes with an eye toward lasting fame. In speaking
about his work, he assumes its universality; he bristles at any suggestion of idiosyncratic or anachronistic concerns. Time is seen as
potentially confirming the value not only of the author's work, but
through that of his knowledge and experience—establishing his worth-
iness in his own eyes, in those of family and friends (whether living
or dead), and in God's eyes. Price also welcomes his work as something to do every day: "given my life," he says, "it was write or choke
in chaos, self-hate."[12] All of his work is an "attempt to seize territory
from chaos,"[13] to structure the experience of his own life. Thus he
constructs both labyrinth and minotaur, the monstrous fear which occupies the "terrible core" of his work—a core which Price describes
as "that small clearing in the jungle which may be empty of all but
a polished mirror."[14] As lens and shield, the fiction allows him both
to confront that harrowing image of the self alone and terrified and
to protect himself from it. Denying that he has written in any literal
form his life story, Price claims that the essential "encounters and
relations" about which he has written had "passed, [were] history and
[lay] in the mind pure as diamond"[15] by the time he was six or seven.
We may assume from this what we learn as easily from the books
themselves, that the fiction of Reynolds Price originates largely (however mysteriously) from his relationship to his parents and from
anxieties experienced in early childhood.

"What I've chronicled," says Price, "is my own world, that world
which has seemed to me . . . to exist *beneath* the world perceived by
other people."[16] The world beneath a world to which Price refers
here is both a personal vision and a religious one. His Christian faith,
Price says, "is one of the two or three central facts about all my work,

maybe *the* central fact. That tragicomic vision of history as creation-fall-redemption-judgement-justice seems to me . . . quite simply, true to observable fact; above all to the facts of my own life."[17] Thus, what may seem an idiosyncratic personal history (that early sense of guilt and fear of disaster) is gathered up in a pattern that is seen as applicable to the lives of all mankind. Price depends upon his Christian faith to supply the comic ending. His work is comic in both senses of that term because he believes that "existence is—or will prove to have been—comic"[18] and because he cares about laughter. Further, surely in part because of his Christianity, Price regards the aim of his work as kinetic; he believes with Rainer Maria Rilke's Apollo that art should cry out to us, " 'You must change your life!' "[19] He thinks that at the "heart" of all literature is "the guarded room in which the poet [has] left his unchained monster, his secret design upon our lives."[20]

The Literary Context

Price has argued that the tracking down of literary influences is generally a wrong-headed and fruitless labor which stems from a serious misunderstanding of the way the narrative imagination works. He believes that where resemblances occur there is usually some common experience to draw upon; "the apples of Cézanne resemble the apples of Chardin"[21] because both men had seen apples. That is his explanation of what early reviewers especially had been sure was the influence of William Faulkner upon Reynolds Price—both men had seen the South. His elaborate syntax is far more likely to have been influenced (if any mimeticism was at work) by the style of seventeenth-century writers like Milton, whom Price studied intently during the period in which his own style was being forged; at that time, and for some years afterward, Price read almost nothing of Faulkner. He did suffer, however, temporary seizure by another great American style: "Michael Egerton," though only that story, sounds like Ernest Hemingway, much more so than any work of Price's sounds like Faulkner.

The "masters" whom Price acknowledges are "the Bible, Milton, Tolstoy, Eudora Welty"[22]—and Hemingway, although his recognition of Hemingway's role came rather late and suggests a psychological rather than a technical importance for Price's own work. Both Milton and the Bible exerted an influence on Price's style; and Tolstoy's

Anna Karenina, the work of literature he admires above all, was consulted for guidance when Price arrived at the sexual scene in *A Long
and Happy Life.* Generally, however, when Price talks about the
writers who have been important to his work, his emphasis is upon
a vision of life that he sees as compatible with his own. In *Things
Themselves* Price discusses the "secret embedded"[23] at the heart of
various literary works, a task which he believes is vital to literary
criticism—and always that secret bears a strong resemblance to his
own.

In "For Ernest Hemingway" Price describes the consolation (the
love and validation) that he and Hemingway have sought to compel
from readers, in exchange for painful stories. He assigns to Hemingway his own "magnetic fields of fear": "simultaneous desperate love
and dread of parents, imagined and actual abandonment by one's
earliest peers, the early discovery that the certified emotions (affection,
love, loyalty) are as likely to produce waste, pain, and damage to the
animal self as are hate, solitude, freedom—perhaps more likely."[24]
The secret that Price finds embedded in *Islands in the Stream* is
"Avoid dependence, contingency."[25] Love is seen as a threat to human
life, because our loved ones betray us by death if not by other means.
If that "certified" emotion (and Price himself certifies love) is not to
occupy our lives, then some other good must be found; for Hemingway, Price believes, *"saintliness"* became a "lifelong subject,"[26] a lure
which implied that virtue could be found in solitude. Price says that
in *Islands in the Stream* Hemingway dealt "with the only one of the
four possible human relations which he had previously avoided—
parental devotion, filial return." It seems significant, given the importance of the relationship between parent and child in Price's own
work, that this relationship—rather than the relation "with God, with
the earth, with a female or male lover or friend"[27]—should yield for
Price the secret of Hemingway's work. Significantly too, the protagonist of that work is an artist whose final lesson (after the death
of his sons) is passed along by Hemingway to Price: *"Prepare, strip,
divest for life that awaits you; learn solitude and work; see how little
is lovely but love that."*[28]

The living writer who seems to have meant most to Price is Eudora Welty. She supplies through her fiction proof that the world and
language Price knew could be used as material for his own work.
Things Themselves contains two essays about Welty which suggest
that the world she shares with Price is not merely the rural South,

but a world in which the operative poles are love and separateness. Price argues that whereas in her early work protagonists often queried their isolation, yearning for life at the other pole, in *The Optimist's Daughter* the position of onlooker is preferred. Love and family are shown as "hurtful, willfully vulnerable, parasitic";[29] communication necessarily fails, because "death and your own final lack of attention doom you to disloyalty."[30] Price concludes that the onlooker's gifts have proved stronger than the lover's: "vision, distance, stamina—the courage of all three."[31] It is exactly the point at which he had arrived in the investigation of Hemingway's work—a defense, in fact, of the solitary artist.

This analysis of Welty's fiction is useful to an understanding of Price's own work, particularly in view of the striking resemblance between *The Optimist's Daughter* and *Love and Work*, written at about the same time. Both novels concern the death of a last surviving parent and lead their protagonists to question the value of love, the damage it may have wrought, and their own exclusion from a vision embraced by the previous generation. While he endorses Welty's preference for the onlooker's gifts, in his own novel Price regards the onlooker in a harsher light; thus his remarks on Welty serve to return us sharply to the balance. This is important because the most common critical misunderstanding of Price's own work has been the assumption that in the polarity between love and separateness he has consistently chosen the former.

Also included in *Things Themselves* are essays about Henry James and William Faulkner, whose "secrets" again—though less central for Reynolds Price than Hemingway's or Welty's—reveal nearly as much about Price as they do about James or Faulkner. The James essay, on *The Wings of the Dove*, suggests that James's "central lifelong obsession"[32] was with betrayal or treachery, often of a sexual kind, where the protagonist is excluded from a love which unites others and which they flaunt in his sight. The Jamesian "demon" of betrayal is also Price's. The Faulkner essay, on *Pylon*, centers on the archetype of "the seductive rascal, the glamorous and lethal tramp." Price remarks that often these "great seducers" possess some "charged" extension "of their superior vitality,"[33] as Faulkner's aviators display their planes—or as Wesley in *A Long and Happy Life* displays his motorcycle. The "hero" figure generally is incapable of returning the love which he compels from the "poet," a fact which Price's own sexual buccaneers "never deny . . . to us."[34] Again we see in Price's analysis of another writer's work a pattern that is apparent in his own; always that pattern relates to the risks entailed by love, and the possibility that the onlooker's position is in the end the more desirable.

What emerges most powerfully from a consideration of Price's connection with other writers is a sense of how adamantine and insistent his own vision is. Such writers have only seen "the apples of Chardin, apples of Cézanne,"[35] as Price has seen them; they have helped less than those figures from his private life who initially revealed to Price the hazards and attraction of the apple itself. For Price, the subject of fiction is not language but life: the apple, in its natural form. Accordingly, he has little patience for contemporary writers like John Barth or Donald Barthelme, who have turned to "the fiction of game and puzzle,"[36] away from the less manageable fascination of how human beings deal with one another. And he admires most those novelists of the nineteenth century or of today who engage as he does "in long watching; slow and incremental description of human lives."[37]

The Southern Context

Although Price has never considered himself a regional novelist, he is undeniably and with sometimes visible pride a Southerner—whose work, moreover, shares a number of important characteristics with that of other Southern writers. Among these are a love of anecdote and colorful speech, a deep attachment to place, and a belief in the importance of the past and of family history. What Louis Rubin has defined as characteristic of the twentieth-century Southern writer is clearly true of Price: "His art has been crafted out of a deep sense of familiarity with the texture of community life, but also of a momentous distancing of himself from that community."[38] That distance can be achieved in a meaningful way only when it has been preceded by familiarity; and what the South has given Price is that chance, the spectacle of human lives deeply entangled with one another, rooted in one place, enduring enough for the author's gaze.

An important fact of Southern life is its persistent rural flavor. For Price, that means the South can provide the artist with a sense of permanence—"objects of meditation, in the presence of which the literally human qualities of his life can be understood, calmed, controlled and shaped."[39] Price believes that contact with the earth itself supplies for human beings, and for the novels they may write, a significant grounding—some assurance of continuity despite our various wanderings and disaffections. He has questioned, in fact, whether "a totally urban novel" is possible at all. The novel, Price remarks, has traditionally "turned on the poles of city and country";[40] and clearly his own work has employed each pole, as well as the tensions between them which are apparent now for any Southerner. Increasingly, Southerners must look back to discover that rural pole. The old way of life—God-and-family centered, rooted in the land—no longer flourishes; "but *surviving*," Price argues, "as opposed to *flourishing* has always been the supreme Southern specialty, black and white."[41]

Most of the qualities we associate with Southern life and fiction are linked to the backward glance, a conviction that the past nourishes, guides, sometimes poisons our present lives. Religion, family history, and the oral tradition all operate in that way as the persistent backgrounding for contemporary life. "The past, as dream, condemnation, cause of the present,"[42] is for Price one grand design which imprints itself in several versions: Christian, Southern, and familial. The Christian doctrine of original sin, for example, has its counterpart in the tragic history of the South and in the family history that has determined so much of Price's fiction. The sin in each case seems to have been pride—which endures, despite guilt. Thus the South is also important for Price as a reflector of human history which is both larger than that (the story of man since Adam) and smaller (the story of Price himself).

Essays, Poems, and Translations

The work that Price has done outside of his fiction confirms resoundingly the insistent nature of that vision which operates within his stories and novels. All of his critical response to other writers returns Price eventually to the subjects and methods of his own fiction; and he manages that without distorting the work of others—his essay on Hemingway, for instance, is unquestionably one of the most valuable ever written. Far more often and more revealingly than most novelists have been willing to do, Price has also published essays exclusively concerned with his own fiction. A third kind of essay to which Price has turned is more general—essays on the South, for instance. All of his essays, as Price suggests in his introduction to *Things Themselves*, are "controlled by the peculiar needs" of his waiting for the fictional muse to come again. They provide in the meantime exercise of allied skills and an opportunity to confront old questions in an arena that matters less.

His poetry also is conspicuously made from the same themes and preoccupations that have been central to the fiction. At the start of his career, however, Price turned away from poetry because it had not become a means of "examining" or "controlling" his experience. The poet's gift, Price believes, is for "verbal intensity," while the novelist's (which he prefers) is for "structural and visual stamina."[43] Less plentiful than the fiction, his poetry is still a considerable achievement. Generally it is narrative: "The Annual Heron," published in *Poetry* magazine in 1979, is a fine example of interest particularly to readers of *A Long and Happy Life*, in which the heron first appeared. Many of the poems are translations, many were privately printed and given to friends at Christmas, and many reveal the author's Christianity more directly than his fiction does.

A Palpable God is a collection of biblical translations from the Old and New Testaments, preceded by a long essay on "The Origins and Life of Narrative." The title of this book and many remarks concerning the goal of his translation are useful to an understanding of Price's style generally. His goal is immediacy, to return us visually to the scene and to release its power, to make God and other mysteries "palpable" to our senses. Price insists that his impulse here and always has been "toward simplicity, clarity, availability."[44] And in fact these translations do possess a startling freshness, an ability to make us feel as Price does that these things must have happened (are happening now) exactly in the way described. Interestingly too, among the passages which Price has chosen to translate are several he has used in the fiction—including the stories of Jephthah's daughter and of Jezebel eaten by dogs, both of which appear in *A Generous Man*. For readers of the fiction, however, the most important message of *A Palpable God* is Price's claim that sacred story is the perfect answer to "the heart's last craving,"[45] that final consolation is to be found only within the terms of that Christian narrative.

The Central Theme

At the heart of Reynolds Price's fiction is a dialogue between love and solitude. Love is seen alternately as the ultimate reward and the largest threat in human life; solitude is both a blessing and a curse. Price has claimed that his work comes "out of a psyche of a person who by either nature or nurture has found himself too independent and desires contingency, who also obviously has extremely complicated feelings about contingency—about the yieldings of freedom that are involved in any of the various brands of contingency."[46] Thus his work contains both passionate testimonials to the importance of love and equally fervent, often shocking disavowals; it honors and blames people of both persuasions, the lovers and the solitaries—and it issues not from an aloof, Olympian perspective which sees and resolves all contradictions, but from a writer who has obvious personal stakes in the question that plagues and generates his work. Possibly because we expect any novelist to choose love, that side of the debate has generally been understood as victorious in Price's work. And it would be easy to find passages to support that conclusion—impassioned, unambiguous speeches; but there is strong evidence of a similar kind on the other side, proof that the dialogue must continue.

Price has described his theme as "an elaborate dialogue" between "free will and compulsion."[47] He questions how far it is possible to escape the fate (the personality) that is laid on an individual by circumstance and particularly by family. As a Christian, he suggests that "one of the meanings of the metaphor of Original Sin" is "the accumulated genetic propensities-to-folly of man." Believing firmly in genetic and early environmental determinism, he also claims that man "both suffers from and is blessed by free will."[48] Freedom might take the form of moving an individual toward love (if he were led in an opposite direction by nature or nurture) or away from it (if he had been guided otherwise). But most often in Price's work freedom is opposed to love; the loss of freedom is the price one pays for love, whether gladly or in bitterness. The loss of love is equally the price one pays for freedom. In that sense, he does believe in freedom as a human possibility, but he believes as well that we can exercise that freedom to make permanent errors. And the idea of a permanent error—nearly always, for Price, a violation of love—may suggest that we are not as free as we suppose, that our decisions finally are assessed by God in terms of an absolute code which we transgress at our peril.

If then, as seems to be the case for Price, one is consigned by family history to solitude and believes that God's code requires us to love one another, what hope remains? Have two kinds of law simply clashed, and is the violator of God's law damned by the circumstances of birth which God himself allowed? One kind of answer is to write books that describe for God and self and a few significant others the quandry in which such a person finds himself. In fairness to self, such books would acknowledge the claims of solitude and reveal the harm that love can do. The solitary author can also praise love, as Price does; he can exercise the faculties that God has given him, trusting that God will understand the solitude such work requires. He can remind all listeners as well that love is not restricted to the love between husband and wife, as Price has done through his emphasis upon odd couples of all sorts—masters and servants, parents and children, aunts and nephews, siblings, friends. He can point, finally, to another odd couple: the love between God and man, which is largely absent in the lives of Price's characters, but which is by implication their final consolation and his.

Style

Although Price is generally seen as a writer for whom style is of paramount importance, his own remarks on that subject amount to a denial. He scorns any use of language as ornament and attempts to be "as lucid and as immediately clear as is compatible with the complexity of the scene."[49] Nevertheless, his style is highly pronounced, unusual, and quite often difficult. The language generally is highly charged, the sentences are elaborate, the metaphors are often startling, and the precise description of all action (whether physical or emotional) often slows us down. Price would not object to that, however: his goal is to force the reader, to shock him into recognition, to create a physical immediacy which gives the reader pause.

Price has claimed that he writes the most Anglo-Saxon prose currently being produced in America and has also defined his style (and that of the King James version of the Bible) as the "paradoxically baroque plain-style."[50] The Anglo-Saxon qualities are what make it plain: an emphasis on concrete words rather than abstract, and a syntax which can be described as paratactic (that is, a cumulative assault, an additive or horizontal syntax, rather than the Ciceronian style which depends much more on subordination). His prose in fact has a muscular, abrupt quality which we associate with Anglo-Saxon; it avoids what Price terms a "treacherous smoothness."[51] Yet there is also undeniably a rhetorical quality, an elaboration which we tend to think of as baroque and which has misled some readers into thinking of Price's style as Faulknerian. While his sentences are often long, they tend to rely upon parentheses and noun phrases to accrete a total meaning, and they lack the quality of suspension found in more typically baroque syntax. Again, the goal is to keep us where we are, to wrench from each phrase of a sentence its immediate impact. Perhaps the most striking feature of this style is its heavy reliance upon a core vocabulary. Most of Price's favored words are Anglo-Saxon rather than Latin in origin, nearly all are common and emotionally charged, and all are words that serve his central themes. Indeed, even a partial list of such words takes us into the heart of the author's vision: *protect, shield, threat, lethal, pain, loss, perfect, permanent, misery, pardon, plea, promise, blame, waste, warn, amends, ruin, error, wish, desperate, receipt, goal, gift, want, need, food, suck,* and *famine.* These words suggest the intensity of Price's concern with human interchange, both the damage it can wreak and the sustenance it may provide.

Those readers who accuse Price of overwriting claim by implication that he takes the complexity or the importance of his material too seriously. They would prefer that intense patches be relieved by something more casual and, in their view, more realistic. Their charge assumes either that his intensity is affected to make himself sound impressive or that if his intensity and complication are genuine they are still excessive. A strong argument, however, against the truth of the former assumption is that Price has demonstrated an absolute commitment to one thoroughly articulated vision. If he were concerned merely with a glossy surface, surely he would have applied that in a more random fashion to whatever matter would accept the glaze. Instead, what we find is a remarkably thorough correspondence between what the style signals and what Price believes about human life, as well as a remarkable concentration upon that set of beliefs. An evaluation of Price's style becomes, therefore, in large part a judgment upon his vision: if that is not excessive or distorted, then his style is not.

Other features of his style include a dense imagistic structure, a narrative voice which is often quite close to the speech of the characters, and considerable humor. Many of the same image patterns are used consistently throughout Price's fiction. Although such imagery (often verging on symbolism) is strikingly apparent, Price says he is "never conscious of symbols"[52] when he is planning or writing a story, and he has a strong aversion to symbol-mongering on the part of critics. Again, what he would dislike is any suggestion of appliqué, of imposed decoration: the image patterns and symbols of his fiction grow naturally (and abundantly) from his diction and themes and from the physical world which Price creates. That same deep unity of fictional elements can be seen in the relationship of narrative voice and dialogue. Often, the narrative voice will echo folk rhythms (avoiding the subjunctive, for instance); at the same time, the dialogue is more literary, more studied and to the point than is strictly credible. Nearly everything the characters say contributes to the author's themes; and there is a strong similarity in tone, diction, and phrasing as we move from one character to another or from dialogue to the narrative voice. Roughly the same kind of humor (both extravagant and deflationary) appears in the dialogue and the narration. Humor functions in Price's fiction as it does in life—as a vital leavening, a delight, and a reminder of true proportions.

Chapter Two
A Long and Happy Life
Introduction and Plot Summary

The situation of the heroine in *A Long and Happy Life* was inspired in part by a Vermeer painting called *Young Woman in Blue Reading a Letter*, which shows its subject pregnant and without a wedding ring. That familiar dilemma is explored by Price in terms of the choice between marriage and solitude, or the need for both a sense of community and a sense of the autonomous self. Wesley Beavers, who sends letters to Rosacoke Mustian, at last offers to marry her—and she accepts, finally. But these delays are not the only obstacles to happiness. Marriage itself, endorsed as the most natural of choices, does not ensure a happy ending. Price sets his novel in a rural place called Afton, North Carolina, and creates there "a circle in the forest"[1] in which to stage the mating games common to pastoral literature. Graced by the charm we associate with pastoral vision, these games do not constitute an escape from the realities of life. Dangers lurk in the deep woods.

The novel is divided into three parts, reflecting the "temptation—sin—redemption"[2] pattern which Price originally intended for the book. Part One is structured around two church functions, one black and the other white, both demanding Rosacoke's attendance. At Mount Moriah is the funeral of her black friend Mildred Sutton, dead from giving birth to Sledge (Sammy Ransom—caretaker for Mr. Isaac, the richest man in Afton—has not admitted his paternity); and at Mason's Lake is the annual picnic of Delight Baptist Church, where Rosa's family and friends are cooling off. She leaves the funeral in pursuit of Wesley, whom she meets at Mr. Isaac's spring; they next proceed to the picnic, where Wesley fails to seduce her. He returns to Norfolk, Virginia, to sell motorcycles and to consort with "hussies." Several months pass, marked only by two painful letters from Rosa to Wesley—in one she asks, *"are we in love?"*[3]—and by the two cards he sends in lieu of adequate reply.

In Part Two, Wesley flies home briefly with Willie Duke Aycock

and her "aviator." Believing that he has left again without seeing her,
Rosa sets out first to visit Mildred's baby and next to the Beavers'
house, to ask Wesley's mother what she has done wrong. Instead
she encounters Wesley, is charmed by his harmonica, and decides to
"hold" him the only way she can. Their "sin" in a broomstraw field
seems its own "redemption" until Wesley thanks Rosa by calling
her "Mae." Letters follow, including a lengthy (and improbable)
epistle in which Rosa describes for Wesley the prelude to her sister-
in-law Sissie's delivery of a stillborn son. Her brother Milo's desperation makes Rosa promise to keep him company, but she abandons him when a new letter from Wesley reveals that what they
have euphemistically called "deer-hunting" has made her pregnant.

Rosacoke is isolated by her secret as Part Three opens. Wesley
has come home for Christmas and not yet come to visit her. He
catches up with her at Mr. Isaac's, to say that she is needed in the
Christmas pageant as a substitute for Willie Duke (whose elopement
completes the comic subplot of a pastoral romance). Wesley learns
of Rosa's pregnancy and suggests that they elope too. Rosa says no
and has until after the pageant that evening to change her mind.
The novel ends with Rosa in the role of Mary resigning herself to
the knowledge that it is her wish as well as her duty to marry Wesley.
The "redemption" is complete.

Space and Nature

If we follow closely the many topographical clues offered by Price,
it becomes clear that he is working hard (by implication, not statement) to create an impression of circular space. A right turn from
the Mustian driveway can serve as our entry to the circular dirt road
along the circumference of which Price has established the principal
settings of his novel. Next after the Mustian place come Mr. Isaac's
house and pond and pecan grove; Delight Church with its graveyard;
the most important stretch of Mr. Isaac's woods, including the spring
and broomstraw fields; Mount Moriah, the Beavers' house, the Sutton
place, and finally the Mustian home again. Other locations in the
vicinity—such as Warrenton (where Rosa works) and Mason's Lake—
are reached by "paving" (4), the one road we know of that leads
out of this enclosed, rural world. To the north is Norfolk, Virginia,
an opposite, significantly urban, and dramatically unrealized pole for
the novel. Wesley shuttles back and forth between Norfolk and

Afton, echoing from Norfolk that alternation with rural locales by his periodic visits to the beach at Ocean View. Farther still is Oklahoma, where Rato is stationed—all we are told, for the farther away we go from Afton the less we know of place.

The repetition of Afton locales and the attention paid to routes and modes of conveyance gradually yield a sense of intimately known space, as well as of restriction. Superimposed upon the present action of the novel, and therefore increasing the density of that space in which it occurs, are a number of remembered scenes. Most of these are like tableaux, repeated several times to convey a sense of history shaped by revelation, and some occur on the road itself. In its circularity the road suggests not only an enclosed space, but also life's road—along which Mildred, for example, must travel the brief fated distance that remains to her. The overlay of remembered scenes, of mental upon physical space, works in two ways. Either Rosacoke will recall an exterior setting that contrasts with her present enclosed position, as when she thinks of Wesley in the pecan tree while sitting in Mount Moriah, and again when she recalls nearly all of the exterior loci of the novel while playing Mary at Delight Church; or she will see through a present exterior setting to recall an event that occurred there, or nearly there. Price also uses the narrator to increase our sense of pictorial density in his world. Thus at the beginning of the novel the narrator describes both what the dust might have settled on some other day, such as Mustians walking to church or Negro children carrying blackberries along the road, and what Rosacoke fails to see that day as she rides to Mount Moriah on Wesley's motorcycle.

One of the most impressive achievements of *A Long and Happy Life* is its evocation of what might be termed the natural surround. The "waiting" land seems animate, almost conscious of some design upon Rosacoke—some gift or threat which it holds in reserve for her. As Wesley's motorcycle speeds toward Mildred's funeral, the dust rises to cover everything, just as in the past it had settled upon black children with their berries and on Emma Mustian's white, but "dusty children" (160). It comes like a harbinger of death, in which individuality is lost; thus it is associated with the grave of Rosacoke's father—which is sinking, and needs to be filled with fresh dirt if the link between Horatio Mustian and those members of his family who remain on the surface of earth is to be preserved. The dust forms a "sudden halo" (9) for Rosacoke at Mount Moriah, perhaps to suggest a more positive view of what waits "on the other side" (7) of the grave or the natural surround. This sense of the dust as somehow valuable is confirmed by an implicit contrast to the "concrete" which is regularly associated with the streets of Norfolk; a kind of spiritual death occurs where human beings lose contact with the earth. Delight Church itself is built on sand under two oak trees, implying some relationship between the Christian (supernatural) and natural worlds, and opposing an image of transiency (sand) with another of permanence (oaks).

As death is thought to creep, so at the end of Part One the dust of the opening is replaced by "frost creeping towards" Rosacoke on the November night when Wesley has failed to visit her. It moves "like hands" over the grass, "reach[ing]" (70) for the house; and the suggestion is plain that life without Wesley is a chilly affair, a kind of death. If the natural surround often seems aggressive in this novel, its intention is apparently as much sexual as deathly. The forces of death and sex are often opposed, but they are also intimately connected—as we know from Mildred's death in childbirth and Milo's stillborn son. Thus, we are made to feel that Rosacoke will die if she does and die if she does not yield to the forces of sexuality.

The "creeping" frost is picked up again at the beginning of Part Two, when on that frosty Sunday morning Rosacoke wakes to see "the road . . . full of black children creeping towards Mount Moriah" (71). Black children in particular, but also the "swarm of humming girls" who are "Messenger Angels" (176) in the Christmas pageant, appear as intermediaries between this world and the natural or supernatural surround. As if from "the other side," they creep and swarm toward a center occupied by white adults. Significantly anonymous, the little black "boys that belonged to most anybody . . . swarmed out" (14) to contemplate the mystery of Wesley's motorcycle at Mount Moriah. This lack of individuality is a major part of the threat that is posed to the ego by sex and death, but it can also be seen as offering transcendence.

Similarly placed on the periphery of the circle are babies and black adults. Babies occupy that position metaphorically, by virtue of premonitions and something like Wordsworthian knowledge of a prior existence. Thus Sledge wakes "from whatever awful place he went to when he slept" (88), and Frederick Gupton (as the Christ child asleep in Rosa's arms) smiles from the "corners of his mouth . . . slow as if they were pulled like tides by the moon" (195). Milo's stillborn son (returned so quickly to the dust) and Rosa's unborn child reinforce our sense of babies as occupying the border between two worlds. Blacks seem to occupy that position more literally. On the fringes of white society, characters like Sammy Ransom are often placed in the dark. And they are often mysterious, like Sammy—or like Landon Allgood, the gravedigger who bears holly from the deep woods to Mary Sutton's house. Of all the human dwellings in the novel Mary's is the most distant from the circular road; "washed by the rain to no color at all ... like a bone the sun sucked out" (86), it is also the most vulnerable to nature's forces.

Landon's paregoric enforces an association of the gravedigger with a kind of netherworld, the sleep of pleasure and death which surrounds ordinary social life, which threatens at Mount Moriah to erase Landon's memory of his kinship to Mildred, which threatens also to sink the grave of Rosa's father unless Landon can summon energy to care for it. The danger of such encroachment is indicated by the fact that one of Landon's drugged stupors ended with his toes freezing and having to be cut off. But vision also can be won by exposure to these forces: thus Landon's strange mistake in thinking that Milo's dead baby was Rosa's can be accounted for as extrasensory perception—he sees the baby in Rosa's womb. Paregoric serves as a link between blacks and babies, indicating their place on the periphery, when Rosa notes that Frederick (doped for the pageant) smells like Landon.

Most conspicuous of these intermediaries circling Afton are the animals—birds, snakes, deer, fish, and so on—who operate principally as messengers to Rosacoke. They are always encountered in the natural world, and usually they are associated with sexuality (and with Wesley). Rosacoke and Mildred in a broomstraw field see a deer which causes Mildred to cry out "Great God A-mighty" (6). What they have experienced is an annunciation, prefiguring the sexual destiny of both girls. They are afraid to continue, and Mildred's early death suggests she had good reason to be afraid. In terms that (like Mildred's cry) may imply access to the supernatural through the natural, they wonder "where *would* they end [these woods], and what would be growing in any field they found on the other side, and who would be tending it there?" (7). A similar impression is gained by the reference later to "whatever it was that sent up those few bubbles from the deepest bottom of the lake" (55).

Rosacoke

Surely for most readers the outstanding achievement of the novel is its characterization of Rosacoke Mustian. We enter fully into the pain of her love for Wesley, her growing isolation, and her sense of liberation when she discovers that she no longer wants him. Whether we approve or rebel against her final decision to marry him, the passionate interest we feel in that decision is a tribute to Rosacoke. She is generous, warm-hearted, romantic and sensitive, and convinces us of what she feels herself: that her life matters, her choices count. She has a strong sense of self, as well as of her duty to others. And she has energy enough to last through long periods of misery.

Her sense of duty is insisted upon from the beginning, as Rosacoke is the only white person at Mildred's funeral. She plays cards when a fourth is needed, worries about leaving dishes in the sink, pays her respects to Mr. Isaac, and fills in as Mary in the pageant. There are lapses certainly, but because Rosa suffers from these we continue to think of her as one whose actions are guided by duty; and we think of Wesley as the force that distracts her periodically from these obligations. More significant, however, is the fact that nearly all of Rosa's flights suggest a fear of maternity. Thus she runs from Sledge and fails to assist in Sissie's delivery. Her abandonment of Milo occurs when she panics at the thought of her own pregnancy. And her flight from Mr. Isaac is really an attempt to evade Wesley, as well as her duty to the child she carries; pointedly, Mr. Isaac insists that she give the candy she has brought him to " 'the children' " (166). The implication is that Rosacoke's duties have changed. Where duty to oneself comes in is a separate and painful issue.

The dominant fact about Rosacoke is her obsession with Wesley. When at the picnic Mr. Mason asks Rosa to cite her favorite biblical text, she answers without hesitation: " 'Then Jesus asked him what is thy name and he said Legion' " (55). The reference is to Mark 5:9, and the man is called Legion because of the many demons who inhabit him. Rosa is similarly possessed by Wesley, twice referred to as "a dozen boys swarming on her" (104); and such possession has interfered with her true identity, her name (just as the man is called Legion). Rosacoke fears the loss of her identity, of all that she has been and might be apart from Wesley; she also fears that he will fail to recognize her. Accordingly, Wesley's great sin is to call her

Mae—in effect to call her Legion, to say she is nothing more particularized than his many "hussies."

Rosacoke's desire not to become utterly absorbed in Wesley is as important to an understanding of her character as the intensity of her love for him. We become aware of this through Rosacoke's frequent efforts to displace Wesley from her consciousness. She is always alert for "something big enough to take her mind off how he looked" (134) or "some new sight . . . to cheer her through the day" (67). The death of Milo's baby, for instance, is "big enough to hold her mind off whatever troubles she had" (127). At church, when Willie shows up with her aviator and Wesley has not appeared, Rosacoke assesses her surroundings and finds "nothing to think of but Wesley Beavers." Then Mr. Isaac arrives, "so she had [him] to watch . . . to take her mind off whatever people were behind her" (74). By "whatever people" she means the possibility of Wesley, which is often the way she tries to keep the image of him at bay— as when she reflects on "whoever else flew with them back to Norfolk" (86).

It is through the workings of Rosacoke's mind that we know her. Other lessons we learn in this manner are that Rosacoke has a passionate desire to be recognized, and that she values experiences all the more if she can claim them as her exclusive property. On the morning when Wesley fails to appear in church, Rosacoke observes Mr. Isaac sneaking candy: " 'I have seen it alone,' " she thinks, " 'so maybe the day wasn't wasted' " (76). Later he gives her a secret smile, revealing the candy clenched in his fist—and Rosa is gratified, "thinking he finally knew her" (77). There are numerous other examples of this quality in Rosacoke, but what emerges from them— as well as from her tendency to look for "signs" which may confirm or guide her choices—is a sense that Rosacoke is very aware of herself as a kind of secret heroine. She has a touchingly dramatic sense of her own life, which may cause us to look with dismay upon the ending of the novel. We are more likely to fear a descent into the ordinary than to suppose that Rosacoke should take it as her just deserts.

What Rosa has been running away from, what reaches out from the natural surround and catches her, is the force of sexuality. There is no suggestion that in giving herself to Wesley she has considered her own erotic pleasure, or indeed that she has been seriously tempted by him in the past. Yet it is obvious that her attraction to Wesley is largely sexual. The author has both Rosacoke's own consciousness and an external perspective available to him, but he chooses to exercise extreme delicacy in the matter of Rosa's sexual feelings. Such reticence strengthens our belief in Wesley's sexual magnetism, for it relies on the principle that what is unstated is most powerfully felt. This strategy imparts to Rosa an aura of freshness, an innocence appropriate to the morning of life; it also suggests a lack of knowledge needing to be filled out, threatening her by the vulgarity of Milo's Santa Claus jingle or promising her (also in Milo's phrase) " 'a lovely future' " (39). These possibilities are not mutually exclusive, as Rosa begins to learn in her initiation by Wesley. Only for a brief time does it seem that her idealism is sustained by lovemaking: "They came so close they broke out in one long 'Yes,' and what he had made, so careful, fell in like ruins on them both" (104). Post-coital sadness (where union begins to seem illusory) is then hideously confirmed as he calls her Mae. Yet the intention of those natural forces has been satisfied: Rosacoke is pregnant, and that seems the ultimate purpose of her desire. She is caught. It does not matter to the forces of anonymity and continuance if he mistakes her name.

Wesley

Wesley Beavers is the principal agent of those forces that invade Rosa's life and lead to her capitulation. Although *A Long and Happy Life* is clearly Rosacoke's book, it is the heat given out by Wesley and felt by Rosa that generates the novel. Indeed, it is hard to think of another book (by man or woman) in which the sexual attractiveness of a young man is so powerfully conveyed. Price accomplishes this through discreet but insistent attention to Wesley's body, through imagery associated with him, through Wesley's distance from Rosacoke, and through the intensity of her longing for him. We also believe in Wesley's sexual magnetism because we cannot otherwise account for Rosacoke's obsession with him. That Wesley should cause Rosa so much pain, seeing and caring so little about it, may well operate as a barrier for our appreciation of him. And Price himself saw a difficulty, even before the novel was begun: "The problem is to make Wesley—for all his insensitivity and callous hunger—somehow a person whom Rc. can, believably, love. The scene when she sees him playing the harmonica will do a good deal to solve the problem . . . Of course, one of her great troubles is that she hasn't fully admitted how much of her love for Wesley is based in desire."[4] Rosa loves him partially because he can be seen as a kind of visionary. When she first observes Wesley, "his eyes . . . stared straight out at sights nobody else in Warren County was seeing unless they were up a pecan tree" (19). He sees smoke, which she cannot; and her attraction is born of this disparity between them, admiration of his vision, and simultaneous regret that it distracts him from attention to herself. Natural as this response is, it signals a potential defeat for them both: if she gets him, Wesley will necessarily descend into mere actuality. Wesley seems poised for flight, and later he will join the Navy, ride a motorcycle, make love with a variety of women—all to exercise that freedom. But Rosa's first, peremptory speech suggests a fated limitation: " 'Boy, shake me down some nuts' " (19). He obeys, seemingly without implicating himself. Later, another and obviously parallel form of Wesley's heedless bounty (also supplied at her request) will attach him to Rosacoke for good.

Echoing this first sight of Wesley is the harmonica scene, which hints at the end of Wesley's freedom. Again Rosacoke intrudes upon his private space. Again he seems to be in a kind of trance, but his vision is now curiously restricted: "Wesley himself was still as a blind man when his guide suddenly leaves him, embedded upright in the gray air like a fish in winter, frozen in the graceful act, locked in the ice and staring up with flat bitter eyes—far out as anything can be and come back" (93). It seems that Wesley's vision has somehow failed, that so long as he had a "guide" (mobility or the belief in his own freedom, perhaps) he was unaware of his limitations; now, though he still yearns with "bitter eyes," he is described as "a blind man" frozen in place. This disappointment significantly precedes (although it may prefigure) his capture by Rosacoke; it lends poignancy and depth to his characterization, for we see that Wesley's original conception of freedom has not been met adequately by his career as a "motorcycle man." As much as the beauty of his music, Wesley's sadness in this scene helps to make him credible as the object of Rosa's love.

As he tells Rosa, Wesley acts out of the necessity of his own nature—" 'Because I am Wesley' " (52). And Price admires him for this: "I like his homogeneity. I like the fact that he's all one thing—which I think men generally are and which women find hard to accept in men."[5] Wesley is good at waiting, to grow up or to see the deer in Mr. Isaac's woods; he can wait single-mindedly without any part of his consciousness fixed on Rosacoke. When the time comes, he is also good at moving. He lives "in the present" (7), whether still or whirling like a dervish on roads and women.

On the one hand, Rosacoke and Wesley are opposed types: "Whereas man is seen as the wanderer, the buccaneer, the rogue, or the faithless one, woman is seen as the faithful passive waiter." This is "the male/female eros" which Price sees in all his work: "man's love is of man's life a thing apart; it is woman's all."[6] And it is true that Wesley as buccaneer exhibits only intermittent interest in Rosacoke. On the other hand, Wesley and Rosacoke can be said to resemble each other. There is a great deal he fails to see or understand in Rosacoke, but Wesley does have a kind of vision that is comparable to hers. On the day of the picnic he has sightings of Rosacoke (as she has of him), and he uses the mules as she does to reflect the stubbornness that prevents their coming together. Like Rosa, he looks for "signs" to guide his action. Each, in fact, has a time for waiting and a time for motion, each retreats from and pursues the other, and each finally is caught.

Wesley's association with the natural forces that invade Rosa's life is relentlessly insisted upon by the imagery. Thus he "swarms" on Rosa's body, and his motorcycle—"'that machine between his legs'" (27)—bears down "to get what it wants or like an arrow for her heart" (85). Well-oiled, limber, and powerful, the bike functions as an emblem of Wesley's sexuality. On it he moves "from inside like a snake" (3), as in making love to Rosacoke he moves "from inside the way he did everything but planned this time fine as any geared wheel, slow at first and smooth as your eyeball under the lid" (104). Fearful of his motorcycle and sexuality, Rosa had in the opening scene "slackened her grip" on Wesley's hips because "it was too much like holding your eye through the lid while it turns, smooth in the socket but easy to ruin" (8). Wesley's mind also works in this smooth, natural way—like a spring. Thus, when he needs to think what to do about Rosa's pregnancy he tries "the only way he knew—by draining his eyes and his mind of everything and waiting till an answer rose to the surface" (168). That Wesley cannot recollect the names of his Norfolk women or Rosa's face when he is in the Navy is likewise a sign of his proximity to the natural surround, the forces of anonymity. His motorcycle is compared to " 'a circular saw' " (42)—Rosa looks as if she has been riding on one, Mama says; and then Milo, referring to Mildred's difficulty in naming a father for her child, says " 'If you back up into a circular saw, you can't name what tooth cuts you first' " (46). This parallel confirms the phallic and mechanical nature of Wesley's bike, its threat for Rosacoke, and the lack of concern for individuality that is implicit in the momentum of sex.

As Wesley's mind works like a spring, so consistently this ex-Navy man who skinny-dips at Ocean View, who swims and dives so beautifully at Mason's spring-fed lake, is identified with the natural force of water. His long dives into the lake are also frightening to those who wait on shore; there is always the possibility of death, of not returning from the natural surround. Rosa is therefore deputized by Mr. Mason as lifeguard for Wesley. Yet water implies continuance, a gift to parched lands and bodies; the spring, muddied and clogged by leaves, will inexorably renew itself. Wesley, who drinks that pure water, likewise offers participation in a natural cycle to Rosacoke, and so the yes which marks her final acceptance of Wesley is described as "boil[ing] up in her like cold spring water through leaves" (195).

After the funeral, Rosa goes to the spring and decides (like Mr. Isaac) to bathe her feet, despite the risk of water moccasins; we recall that Wesley has been associated with snakes. She gazes at her bare legs and thinks, " 'you're saving it, honey, till the right time comes' "—at which point Wesley fortuitously arrives, "stroking through the branches like a swimmer" (35). At Mason's Lake he cavorts with Willie Duke—whose breasts are " 'God's own water wings' " (44)—and surfaces from a long dive "holding a handful of bottom overhead as proof" (43) of his profound, implicitly sexual experience. Wanting to make love to Rosa, Wesley says he is "thirsty"—a metaphor, obviously, since he is " 'standing in several thousand gallons of spring water' " (56). Just as the buck will lead his does to water, so Wesley now takes Rosa's hand and heads into the trees in search of "drinking water"; they look at the ground "as if a deep well of water might open at their feet," establishing the connection with Mr. Isaac's spring. " 'Maybe it ain't water I'm looking for' " (58) Wesley says. In any case, he fails and returns to Norfolk—where Rosa sends a letter indicating that the ponds have dried up in his absence. When

at last they do make love, Wesley is described as "oaring her as if he
was nothing but the loveliest boat on earth and she was the sea that
took him where he had to go" (104).

The animals of the novel are likewise associated with Wesley.
Negative examples include the hornet (last of a swarming hive) who
may be lingering in the nest at Mount Moriah, "getting older and
meaner" (11) as Wesley might; and the fish locked under ice in
the harmonica scene; and the urine-colored goat's head stain on
Rosa's ceiling, a seeping inward of the natural surround which is
linked to Wesley as the Pan figure whose music soon will charm her
from such misery. Of more positive examples, the deer is most conspicuously linked to Wesley. He leaps on his bike "like a deer" (21),
and Rosa mocks herself for examining Wesley's motorcycle tracks
like " 'an Indian nosing out a deer' " (28). Wesley is associated with
the black-eyed deer which in the annunciation scene with Mildred
stays so briefly that the little girls cannot "say if it had horns" (7),
and with that other deer who appears first so briefly that Wesley—
echoing both Mildred's "God A-mighty" and the "Sweet Jesus" of
black women in church or of his Norfolk women making love—
must tell Rosa that he had horns, was surely male. Wesley is charac-
teristically interested in how many does this buck will lead to water;
seeing Wesley wait, Rosacoke thinks " 'him and that deer are something similar' " (99). Other animals we may associate with Wesley
as traveler are the blacksnake moving "deeper in the trees," of whom
Rosa asks " 'Well, old brother, which way are *you* headed?' " (29),
and the cardinal headed north to Virginia whom she reproves for
" 'looking so biggity,' " warning him (as she might Wesley), " 'You
better stay in North Carolina, boy. You are the official bird here' "
(30).

"You could joke with a cardinal all day long," Rosa thinks later,
"but what did you say to something like a hawk?—nothing that the
hawk would answer." This elusive hawk she encounters "riding" on
Wesley's harmonica music is "a killing bird" (91). Its association
with Wesley is subtly enforced by the way lesser birds (at Mount
Moriah and when Rosa is at the spring) are suddenly still as Wesley
approaches; by the guinea hens which scream, causing Rosa (troubled
by Wesley) to think " 'It must be a hawk troubling them' " (144);
and by the description of Wesley's perching like "the eagle on
money" (19) in the pecan tree. The hawk's "fine-boned wings met
under him in a thrust so long and slow that Rosacoke wondered if

they wouldn't touch *her*—his wings—and her lips fell open to greet him, but he was leaving, taking the music with him and the wind" (91). Rosa is compelled not to let that happen, and so she proceeds to Wesley's house—to face the music.

Clearly, Rosa is in the position of Leda here—as Mildred was when her "mouth fell open" (6) to greet the deity, or as the cow was when " 'that plane touched ground, [and] every tit on the cow stood out like pot legs and *gave'* " (68). As Wesley approaches Rosa in the pageant, again "her head rolled back and her lips fell open as if she would greet some killing bird" (188). Wesley was conceived as "a kind of Ananké looming over and finally crushing Rc.,"[7] and "Ananké," in Greek religion, was a personification of compelling necessity or ultimate fate. Long after the publication of the novel Price made this claim for Wesley: "He says: 'Because I am Wesley.' Wesley has that slightly godlike quality, you know—God tells Moses that His name is I AM."[8] Thus Wesley's motorcycle is a "Chariot of God" (14). If Wesley is a kind of animal deity (Leda's swan) approaching mortal woman, he is also parallel to the Holy Spirit (the dove) which impregnates Mary, played by Rosacoke in the pageant.

Other Characters

Mr. Isaac Alston is probably the most enigmatic figure in the novel. As one who seems unable to die, as proprietor of the woods and spring, donor of earthly goods, poser of searching genealogical questions, and recipient of elaborate respect and duty from the folk of Afton, he seems a kind of patriarch or presiding deity for his people. Yet he is seriously impaired, paralyzed on one side so that he appears to have a line drawn straight through his middle. And he is a child again, for whom candy is all-important. His paralysis, moreover, reflects an atrophy of the heart and body caused by his bachelor state: there is "a shield" (75) on his heart for the simple reason that no one ever asked to marry him. So it would appear that Wesley is lucky to have had Rosa tell him to shake down those nuts from Mr. Isaac's "thinning pecan grove" (71).

Between Mr. Isaac and Wesley, Price has constructed what he terms a "secret arch."[9] There is little obvious connection between these characters, yet Wesley is in a sense both Mr. Isaac's antagonist and his heir. The color tan—of Wesley's Pontiac, the hawk, the dust, and

so on—connects him to Mr. Isaac, whose suit is tan; the movement
only of Isaac's hands, like Wesley's when he plays the harmonica,
is another link. Visiting Mr. Isaac's pond and recalling the summer's
drought, Rosa sees that his "rotten boat" has been swamped by the
"recent rain" (143). That rain, metaphorically, is related to the
"rain" and "hail" of pecans that fell some years before for Rosa and
Wesley, and the "recent rain" is more particularly their lovemaking
which defeated that "drought" of Wesley's first attempt. Wesley's
"loveliest boat" (104) is therefore a contrast to Mr. Isaac's sterile,
rotten boat—and symbolically defeats it.

Two sets of allusion are operating here. Mr. Isaac is like the Fisher
King, who is maimed or impotent and whose land suffers drought as
a result. This association is strengthened by Mr. Isaac's stocking his
pond with fish whose "dim descendants" (5) are the "cold slow-
blooded fish" (163) he hopes to catch. In that configuration, Wesley
then appears as the youthful, questing knight who with phallic lance
seeks the grail. The wasteland is miraculously made fertile by the
rains this quester brings; renewal is accomplished as youth succeeds
age, as spring follows upon winter. Wesley, although a fish locked
under ice (an image connecting him to Isaac), in the end functions
as redeemer. The other external reference is to the biblical Isaac, for
whom the ironic patriarch of Afton is clearly named. Price stirs our
memory of that story by calling one of his churches "Mount Moriah,"
which was the site of Abraham's intended sacrifice of Isaac. The
parallel between the two Isaacs seems especially apt if we recall that
in old age Isaac was a rich man whose fortunes were reversed by
drought and restored by his diligent search for wells.

Mr. Isaac, however, only bathes his feet in the spring. And he lives
in a stuffy house, which seems designed to deny life, with only a
half-crazy maiden sister and Sammy Ransom. But if half of Mr. Isaac
is dead, the other half is not. He seems inclined, perhaps as a consequence of his invulnerability, his removal from the generative
stream, to live forever. Mr. Isaac's own attitude to death is curiously
mixed: he hopes to outlive his father, yet would pray for death if
he thought it were possible for him to die. What Price seems to be
hinting at is a choice between the sexuality that leads to death, on
the one hand, and isolation (a living death) on the other. Isaac can
also be seen as an early version of the solitary artist figure in Price's
work—one whose life choice precludes the usual sort of love for himself, but who nevertheless preserves attachments to the community, to

his original family, and to the idea of what has been denied to his own life.

Milo has made an opposite choice, which has not turned out well for him. Once a sensitive boy, the new and inferior Milo (in Sissie's orbit) suggests a coarsening of sexuality, a vulgarity which lies on the other side of experience and in which Wesley participates to some degree. Their camaraderie seems composed largely of this and a desire, on Milo's part especially, to hold onto a feeling of youthful freedom. Milo is obviously a person in some pain, even before the loss of his child: he is aware of having lost something in himself, of having settled for less than he had intuited as possible. Naturally, he tries to escape this knowledge—by exaggerating the importance of raw sexuality, the one part of "a lovely future" he has left, and by a sense of himself as realistic, the hardness which comes out in his attitude to Mildred's death. Milo's philosophy, " 'Nothing happens to people that they don't ask for' " (51), is basically self-accusatory, an effort to stamp out his own last fragments of a dream.

Most of the males in this novel are linked to Wesley in some fashion. Milo, for instance, slept in the same bed with Rosacoke until he got his driver's license (an indication of dangerous sexuality parallel to Wesley's motorcycle). Milo's hair, tan or the color of broomstraw, also links him to Wesley. As Milo provides an example of the male caught by impregnating a woman, so Sammy Ransom—whom Milo describes as " 'the nigger [that] killed Mildred Sutton' " (46)—illustrates the possibility of evading that responsibility. Also obviously linked to Wesley is Rosa's father, from whom Milo got his broomstraw hair. In the "tan" photograph which Mama shows to Rosa, her father is shown at Ocean View (Wesley's territory) as a "serious" boy—like Milo originally, or like Wesley in the pecan tree—who had " 'nothing but the way he looked' " (84). Similarly, Wesley's face is "his real gift" (188). Shut off from a male world, Rosa and Mama wonder what the smaller boy in the photo might be saying to Rosa's father, just as Rosa cannot hear what Wesley's little brother is saying in the parallel harmonica scene. Rosa's father, Mama tells her, had " 'no more will power than a flying squirrel' "; he changed from a serious boy to a drunk who " 'filled [her] up with four big babies and himself to the brim with bootleg liquor and then walked into a pickup truck' " (84). Mama does not offer this tale as a way of dissuading Rosa from Wesley, however—for she asks, " 'What else is there but Judgment Day?' " (85). All men are Wesleys.

Nearly all of the characters serve to illustrate choices made on the critical issue of mating or reproduction. Mama is one for whom duties to children and spouse are clearly paramount, in spite of the hardships and pain she knows so well. Mildred is "killed" by her decision, and Sissie is almost killed by hers. For the first half of the novel Sissie's hypochondria is comic; but when the agony of childbirth overtakes her, and the outcome makes it all seem futile, she becomes a pitiable figure. Sissie joins Mildred as a victim of woman's biological fate. Baby Sister is a maternal sort, hugging and dressing her dolls, including "a daughter-doll who worked and one evening came home to tell her mother she had lice" (82); the "lice" here foreshadow that affliction that Rosacoke, a working girl who becomes pregnant, fears to bring home to Mama. Baby Sister's fate is also shown by her interest in the songs to be played at her wedding and in the hordes of Gupton children who surround her. Gupton babies come out of Marise as easily as "puppies," but they deplete and exhaust her nonetheless—a fact which seems to have escaped Macey, her proud and foolish husband. Another member of the Gupton clan, Arnold—*"the bachelor with no palate"* whom *"they don't show ... off much"* (112)—sits aloof from the family circle and so reminds Rosa of her brother Rato. When Milo teases his mildly retarded brother about getting sex instruction in the Army, Mama says " 'Some folks don't want to get married, do they, son?' ", and Rato answers, " 'I'm one of *them*' " (152). Willie Duke, however, travels the novel's more accustomed path by capturing her man. It seems, then, that those who choose not to marry are somehow impaired, while those who mate do so at the risk of ordinariness and death. In the resolution of the novel Price directs his heroine toward the latter choice.

The Resolution

Part Two of the novel ends with Rosacoke learning from Sammy Ransom that what she saw as a gift to Wesley was also something she took. Effectively, Sammy ransoms her, moves her from "sin" to "redemption" by reminding Rosacoke when he says " 'I thought you had a *good* hold of him' " (146) that she chose to hold Wesley. At first Rosa thinks this means she is entirely to blame for her pregnancy; but Wesley later will tell her that the baby is " 'Not a *hundred* per cent yours' " (171). The recognition of shared responsibility, together with an acceptance of her wish to hold Wesley, will finally end Rosacoke's isolation and restore her to a place in the community. Part Three, however, is a chronicle of Rosa's resistance. It moves slowly, surely through a series of denials, with the narrator sustaining a network of images which can account for Rosa's ultimate reversal. Often in the novel the narrator points to contingencies, to what might have happened (or happened sooner) if something else had not impeded it. Perhaps the most striking example of this is the heron that appears just before Wesley begins his offer: "So both of them failed to notice the one thing that might have helped—rare as lightning in late December, a high white heron in the pond shallows . . . a neck for a moment curved lovely as an axe handle to follow their passing, then thrust in water for the food it had lacked since morning" (169). The "lightning" helps to make this heron seem a miraculous benediction, recalling the thunder and rain associated with Wesley; with the axe—linked to Wesley's face as a "knife" (188) or "weapon" (165) against her—it also suggests a "lovely" hazard in the natural domain where Leda meets her swan. The heron goes fishing in Isaac's pond, looks to water for its food, as Wesley and Rosa have done; it also looks at them, as the deer had—suggesting that nature has a stake in their common venture. If Rosa and Wesley had seen the heron, it would have revealed an auspicious fact: that they might share occasionally in such privileged moments.

Wesley's offer begins with his voice "almost happy" (169), a statement that his debts are paid, that marriage now " 'don't upset my plans too much' " (171), and a strong suggestion that Wesley is interested in the fate of ordinary mortals which has overtaken him. We take satisfaction in Rosa's emphatic counterclaim that she is " 'not *everybody*' " (171), in her refusal orchestrated to coincide with the instant of Wesley's dwindling into an ordinary, rather appealing young man. Their positions are reversed as Rosa sees that "the distance between them—the space—was half what it was" on the evening they made love, and that his face "offered up towards her like a plate" for food had "nothing on it that she wanted, not any more." She feels free, "as if her life was hers" (175).

Rosacoke approaches Delight Church with "her hips like stainless rods, steady and lovely (even now, toting their new burden) as if she was walking towards a prize" (174). This tableau echoes one at the steps of Mount Moriah, where Wesley had seen Rosa "roll her hips . . . letting loose all the power she had there (which was enough to grind rocks)" and wondered "how much of that could he just walk

up and ask for and get" (11). Sexually, he has possessed her—so that
Rosacoke's withdrawal "towards a prize" for the refusal of his offer
seems a fine, ironic comeuppance. Yet the description of Rosa as a
powerful, erotic machine recalls Wesley's motorcycle and hints at
their suitability for one another.

Before Rosa can enter the church, there is a brief scene with Landon
Allgood that suggests Rosacoke's life is not her own exclusively. Like
the sighting of Rosa on the steps, it is a framing device since Rosacoke
had encountered Landon also at Mount Moriah. There he was sleeping off the effects of paregoric, and here Wesley triumphs over Rosa's
wish to make Landon a private gift of a dollar for his paregoric by
offering two dollars as a gift from them both. Landon's appearance,
"with both arms full of holly—thorned leaves and berries that shined
at her . . . like cardinals" (171), recalls his alliance with the natural
surround and particularly Wesley's link to that red bird she had urged
to stay at home. This encounter also leads Rosa to offer *"something"*
(173) to Wesley, the date of Sledge's birth and his name. That she is
compelled to break her silence to Wesley in defense of a baby is a
foreshadowing of her final choice.

Landon's holly is a gift to Mary Sutton, to pay for his dinner, just
as the money for paregoric is repaid by attention to Horatio Mustian's
grave. The holly is intended, Landon thinks, really for Sledge—as
Christmas presents, descending from gifts to the Christ child, essentially are for "the children" to whom Isaac would send the candy.
Throughout the novel, in fact, and culminating in the gifts of the
Wise Men at the pageant, Price has employed the language of giving
and of fair exchange, with a special emphasis on what is owed to
children. Rosa brings stockings for Mildred's birthday and finds her
dead; Milo pays money for eggs at Mary's house, and she remarks
that the clothes for Sledge were payment enough; the Mustians respond to Mr. Isaac's generosity with their annual candy; the community honors his retirement with a valuable wheelchair, which he
may not want or need, but which makes him weep; sex, what Milo
calls " *'old Santy Claus'* " (80), is Rosa's gift to Wesley; and Rato
returns only to play " 'Santa Claus' " (151) with a sack of presents,
the one Baby Sister opens having been meant for Milo's baby. Gifts
may misfire, or the exchange be out of balance, but the process of
giving and receiving must continue. Thus Rosacoke's satisfaction that
Wesley has learned at last how lonely it is " 'donating things to people
that they don't need or even want' " (175) will have to be modified.

The gift she made to Milo, her company which she then withdrew, will be completed in her gift to Wesley, her acceptance of his gift, and the gift both offer of a name for their unborn child.

A strand of imagery which culminates in the pageant is the use of light to reveal the individual and dark to indicate the unknown, a region of sexuality and mystery in which the ego is submerged. In the lovemaking scene Wesley had said he could do without light; and Rosacoke had feared she would not know "just who she was giving up to" (103) or that Wesley might be "keeping company in the dark with whatever pictures his mind threw up" (104). Afterwards, however, Wesley had cast his flashlight up to the stars, saying that the light would never stop—a suggestion that the consequences of their act would go on forever, and that a vision of human continuance can begin in the darkness which seems to threaten it. Going in pursuit of Milo, Rosa had taken a flashlight and then turned it off, "knowing he spoke best in the dark" (131). At Mr. Isaac's pond she had asked the night air " 'What must I do?' ", and Sammy's lantern had instantly appeared "like an answer" (144) from that darkness; she plumbed it by "staring inward at what Sammy Ransom had showed her (not knowing what he did)" (147). Milo, Wesley, and Sammy find some protection in the dark—a chance to hide from claims made on them as individuals; but there is also a suggestion that darkness is where the answer begins.

Further implications of this pattern become clear at the pageant, as one candle after another is ignited to form a "ring of light" (177) which gradually takes over from the "pitch-black air" (176). This "ring" is the circle of Afton society, from which Rosacoke feels excluded by her dark secret. Its light weakens at the edge where Mr. Isaac is stationed following his retirement; behind Isaac is "Sammy in the dark with all he knew" (180). Most of the faces are also illumined singly by candlelight—framed by darkness, as the buck was in Wesley's sudden headlight. Darkness surrounds the individual and the group alike. In isolation, these faces reveal an abiding solitude; they give nothing to Rosacoke of the recognition she so desperately needs. What Rosa wants is a face lit up for her, one that looks at her and knows her and offers its light as a means of guiding her back into the circle. Only Wesley offers that, not protection from the surrounding darkness, but "a chain" (195) that draws her into community nonetheless. Finally, Price suggests, the darkness will be pierced utterly by the resurrection and the light that begins with the

star of Bethlehem: *"Darkness flies, all is light"* (192). The stream of
generation, however, illuminated by Wesley's flashlight in the broomstraw field, is one human way of reflecting all that Christ's nativity
promises for the future.

Yet another long chain of imagery which leads into the resolution
is concerned with names and faces. This also hints at a Christian
dimension of the novel, as at Mount Moriah the blacks sing " 'Precious
Name, Show Me Your Face' . . . meaning it, looking up at the roof to
hornets' nests and spiders as if it might all roll away and show them
what they asked to see" (15). The desire to know God, to establish
mutual recognition with Him, is on another plane what Rosa desires
in seeing and being seen by the deer or Wesley; it is a wish to defeat
the barrier that separates alien beings. Often when names are spoken
or faces consulted to determine whether communication has been
achieved, the answer is disappointing. Names and faces are sometimes
forgotten, and faces are often turned away: thus the individual is
threatened with annihilation, with being effaced from human memory.
Aunt Mannie Mayfield combats this in naming "the fathers of all her
children, far as she could recall" (11); by the time of Mildred's
funeral, however, she has forgotten everyone. If names and faces are
talismans, tokens of the identity we wish to reveal and preserve, they
are also proof of our connection to other human beings—particularly,
of course, our parents.

At the pageant Rosacoke thinks her baby, which she had hoped
would look like Wesley and have his name, will have "no name but
Mustian" (179). She looks at Sammy's face for "some sign that would
prove his part in Mildred's baby" (180), and she examines other
faces for confirmation of who she is, without finding any. Wesley's
face then comes toward her as both "gift" and "knife" (188) so that
she turns to Frederick Gupton—reciting his name, parentage, and
facial characteristics like a charm to ease her spirit. But she has chosen
the wrong diversion, as in the next meditation upon Frederick she
imagines his conception in the faceless dark, after "a cooling storm"
and presided over by "the rain frogs" (193) which had attended her
early meetings with Wesley. She moves on to observe Frederick's
pulse beating, "filling him sure as an unlabeled seed with all he
would be, the ruins he would make and the lives" (193)—just as Wesley's face had "swarmed with warning of the ruins and lives he would
make" (188). Then she thinks of Frederick in a pecan tree or making a " 'child that would have his name and signs of him and the girl

all in its face—maybe even signs of Marise and Macey' " (193–4). Through her creation of interchangeable lives for Wesley and Frederick, and implicitly for the child in her womb, Rosacoke moves toward the yes she speaks to Wesley through Frederick, which echoes the final yes of their lovemaking scene. It is an affirmation of the common human experience, a recognition that we strive for individuality against powerful odds.

The elaborate imagery of the novel supports this interchangeability of men, women, and babies by connecting members of each group to one another. The pageant itself, with its rotation schedule for parts, with the ease of substitution it allows, suggests that even Rato can play a Wise Man, that any young woman will do for Mary, and that any infant (even one as homely as Frederick) can be the Christ child. Opposed to all this is Rosa's insistence that she is "not *everybody*," her wish not to be confused with a swarm of Mae's, her passion, in fact, to be recognized as a unique individual. But the opposition is not a simple one, for Price suggests that identity may be discovered also through the group. If Rosa loses something of her proud individuality by marrying Wesley, she also gains access to those profound and ordinary experiences of connection that have sustained so many human lives.

What she yields to finally is the child sucking at her breast. It is to this child, who might be anyone's, that Rosa speaks her universal yes and to whom she wishes "a long happy life" (195). This willingness to let Frederick suck means that she has finished running from babies, those "loads" and "burdens" taken by women from men; even now the child in her womb is "using her blood for its own" (185), just as Mildred's baby had "suck[ed] blind at her life" (33). The word "life" is often used in this way, as when a leech was seen "pulling hard at Wesley's life" (45). Babies are leeches, threats to the strength and life of women; Rosa, though she has run in her own way as fast as Wesley, is now attacked by two of these parasitic creatures—Frederick and her own baby. But as Marise could smile through her exhaustion at Frederick, so now Rosa yields to him with some pleasure. Babies do need food, after all—and this one is only being pacified. At Mildred's funeral, a baby who dropped his pacifier in the coffin had to be nursed off to sleep so that his cries would not disrupt the ceremony. Rosa had not liked Wesley's postcard of a baby with a pacifier, sent in response to her complaint that she was more than " 'a doll baby that didn't need nothing but a nipple in her mouth' " (59). The caption of Wesley's card reads "*I am A Sucker for Entertainment*" (65), implying that sexual needs count, too, and that Rosa had better attend to them if she wants to attach Wesley to herself. Men and women also are bound to one another from need, and Rosa's response to Frederick—part dire necessity, part joy—can express at the same time her answer to Wesley.

The question, finally, is whether Rosa's future with Wesley is likely to bring her much happiness. The verse of "We Three Kings" which is allocated to Wesley is not encouraging: "*Myrrh is mine, its bitter perfume/ Breathes a life of gathering gloom./ Sorrowing, sighing, bleeding, dying,/ Sealed in the stone-cold tomb*" (188). Moreover, while she is still denying him, Rosacoke has a powerful vision of the life she would endure in Norfolk if she married Wesley: " 'strong pork liver . . . would be all he could afford,' " and there would only be city people who " 'hate each other' " (180) to see from her lonely window. Love—the last word of the book, what Frederick seems to know in his sleep—cannot lend its grace to her picture. But especially if Wesley knows her in more than the biblical sense, there is hope that some of the changes which will inevitably occur for them both may be satisfying. There will be days, as there are for most people, that validate the misery of Rosacoke's vision, but there may also be days when they see the heron together. What Rosa had hoped for herself, "a long life together—him and me," in which they would "be happy sometimes" (179), is therefore neither precluded nor assured by the ending of the novel. Longevity, obviously, cannot be assumed—especially by a pregnant woman; thus Rosa's wish of " 'a long and happy life' " (26) for Mildred came too late. But there is a chance of some blossoming among the thorns of Rosa's marriage, and the certainty of release from "the stone-cold tomb" in a life thereafter. As Mary, symbolized in Dante by the rose, she holds that promise at her breast.

Style

A Long and Happy Life has often been described as a simple tale. Given the extraordinary density of images in this novel, the subtleties of theme which emerge from those image patterns, and the elaborate control Price exerts over such matters as the deployment of characters and settings, that judgment seems remarkably dim. But the accomplishment of this first novel is all the more striking for its ability to elicit that response—not that such a response is adequate, but that it reflects the author's easy and mature handling of his materials. The text is not difficult in any obvious way. It can appeal to us through Rosacoke especially, and through the charm and humor which touch nearly all of the characters and incidents of the novel, without insisting upon the deeper reaches of its design for simple clarity or interest. Once that design is penetrated, however, its elaboration may seem—in critical analysis, at any rate—to overwhelm the surface of the text. And it is important to recall that babies and white herons are themselves before they are anything more ponderous. At Mount Moriah, for instance, when the little boys ask of Wesley's motorcycle " 'What do it burn?' and he [tells] them 'Coal' " (14), we should appreciate Wesley's humor before we ask whether coal is coke, meaning that Rosa*coke* is the fuel Wesley needs. When so many rifts are loaded with ore, it is difficult to know where the mining ought to stop—but there is not much point in turning our backs on simple daylight either.

To mediate gracefully between the surface and depths of his story, Price has developed a remarkably flexible narrative voice. This voice incorporates features of the idiom his characters speak, so we are told, for instance, that "Mama and them" (52) left the picnic. It is also capable of delivering what might crudely be described as poetic effects which are beyond the range of his characters. At the same time these characters speak with more consistent wit and charm than may be thought credible—especially by readers who are not familiar with Southern speech; even those who are will recognize that Price has very capably gilded the lily, without destroying its natural scent. The effect of this gilding (which also involves thematic appropriateness in the dialogue) is to increase our sense of a continuum that exists between the characters and the narrative voice. Sometimes the voice is so close to Rosa's that we cannot tell whose thoughts are being transcribed, while at other times the narrator's perceptions are clearly distinct—and more penetrating than anything the characters can know. This voice, finally, is our guide to the deeper reaches of the novel, our means of access particularly to the natural and supernatural dimensions of a social world.

Many of the sentences are beautifully protracted, lifting us through space or through a series of images, complicating and resolving themselves, depositing us breathless at the close. An obvious example of this type is the novel's first sentence, describing Wesley and Rosacoke on the motorcycle, which is both a clarion call announcing the start of an important career and a careful prelude to the novel as a whole. Often these sentences read like miniature narratives, complete with their own tensions; syntax supplies suspense and then resolution. The quality of artifice is not irritating here, nor is it discordant. The elegance of such sentences in fact is appropriate to the golden world of pastoral which is a part of the novel's design.

Early Dark

The delicate balance of *A Long and Happy Life*, its measuring of "ruins" against "lives," is newly assessed in the play called *Early Dark* which Price wrote some nineteen years later. Many of the decisions he made in *Early Dark* can illuminate the earlier work, although Price warns in his Preface that "the play is not the novel dramatized . . . [for its action is] seen by a different man who stands elsewhere and sees otherwise."[10] Still, the characters and plot are essentially the same, and large chunks of the novel find their way into the dialogue. What happens is that Price alters the affective structure of the novel—changes the lighting, as it were—to let us see what many readers of *A Long and Happy Life* had missed.

In large measure *Early Dark* serves to reveal the author's growing support of Wesley and his belief that Rosacoke is a flawed heroine, attitudes which have been exposed over the years in numerous interviews. Wesley in the play is considerably more attentive to Rosacoke, and therefore less culpable. Rosa simply expects too much—or more, anyway, than she has a chance of getting. Closed off in a room above her family, she is accused of living in a dream world and of valuing herself too highly. Milo and Sissie call Rosa "her Highness" (7) and "Miss God-in-Heaven" (57); Rato says she is "hard on people . . . We're not as quick as you" (106); Wesley reminds her that she is not "the only human made out of skin" (126), meaning he has feelings too; and Mary says "most people lie down and *die* without . . . the love you're talking about" (93). As these voices form a chorus to chide Rosa, so the play's title—like the end of *A Generous Man*—tells us that the ideals of youth are soon eclipsed. Such grim necessity receives endorsement from the author, as if one prisoner would scold another for complaining of their common plight. Wesley, stark naked *"to punish and tempt her"* at the end of the picnic scene, challenges Rosa to make a decision: "you ever know that you really want me—not a dream about me but a person you can see and touch: *not you*—you let me know" (51). She bears a responsibility, then, for her own choice. But the alternative, Price suggests, is endless, onanistic mirror-gazing: to escape the prison of the self, she must accept the prison of others.

Chapter Three
The Names and Faces of Heroes

Reynolds Price's second published book is one of his two collections of short stories. It contains seven pieces that range from his first completed story ("Michael Egerton") to the title story that resolves the collection by reiterating images and themes from the preceding works.

"A Chain of Love"

This story—written before *A Long and Happy Life*—marks the first appearance of the Mustian family in Price's fiction. Milo has just married Sissie, Rato is not yet in the army, and Papa is still alive—although the occasion of the story, a trip to the Raleigh hospital, suggests that Papa's death of "a tired heart"[1] is imminent. Papa's main concern is just to die at home as promised—in contrast to Mr. Ledwell, whose early death in hospital is the major event of the story. Emma Mustian is worried at "not being able to stay [after the drive to Raleigh] when staying was her duty, but they were having a Children's Day at the Church that coming Sunday." It would appear that Emma's duty to Papa is eclipsed by her obligations to youth, but Rosacoke and Rato are "dying to sit with him anyhow" (4), and Mama will be able to take her turn on Sunday. Respect for age and its cares, together with nurture of the young, suggests a deeply interdependent community—a chain of love, in fact, to which Rosa adds further links in the concern she shows for the Ledwells.

As in *A Long and Happy Life* Rosacoke has two interests: Wesley and everything else. If these interests seem opposed, it is also true that Wesley—or his supposed resemblance to the Ledwell boy—serves as the first link in the chain that binds Rosa to the Ledwells. Rosacoke is herself a credible adolescent version of the novel's heroine, for whom love of Wesley made other duties increasingly difficult to fulfill. She is happier here, able to sing and explore the forbidden world of cosmetics. She is only slightly, nicely vain; given to undressing in closets, to a sense of ritual and propriety; and jealous

40

of Papa's nurse, sure that she does more. As with Mr. Isaac in the novel, Rosa is anxious to be known by the Ledwells and to possess her knowledge of them in secret.

In spite of Rosa's efforts to make a home in Papa's room and later to extend her benevolence toward the Ledwells, the hospital itself is "Hell" (23). Beyond its walls, visible to Rosa from the room Mr. Ledwell will occupy, is a statue of Christ—assurance that on the other side of suffering there will be peace. Christ's presence remains in the story, appearing again in Rosa's memory of the Phelps boy who came back from the dead and in our awareness of Christ as healer. The quantity of human suffering, apparent to Rosa in the ward, makes her think "there ought to be something you could do for such people" (23), but she realizes—as Christ warned that the poor will be always with us—that bringing ice water to so many "would be like trying to fill up No-Bottom Pond" (24). And besides, they might not want water. The closed, personal nature of human experience is indicated again by the Phelps boy's keeping a "secret between him and his Jesus" (28). The desire to help others may be defeated by the sheer mass of suffering or by its final secrecy. This paradox may underlie the story's title, for love becomes a chain when it binds one to the suffering of others, if that suffering cannot be relieved. Price uses the imagery of light and dark to suggest how Rosacoke is drawn into a community of suffering. She senses the pain of Ledwell's son, but she is struck by light and retreats like a snail drawing "itself back, hurt and afraid" (26). Later, as the last rites are being administered to Mr. Ledwell, she is drawn on by candlelight (and the face of Ledwell's boy) to be a silent witness. And finally, in Papa's room, her "voice cut through all the dark" (42) to express her grief at Ledwell's death.

The soft light in Ledwell's room reveals to him the sad face of his son, which seems to keep him from dying; when that light goes out, Price suggests, the wall separating Ledwell from Christ will be dissolved. His "living picture" (42), however, will remain in his son; and Ledwell has done his best to ensure continuity, to pay his debts in this world, by reminding the boy " 'to give Jack Rowan one of those puppies' " (39). He says this instead of "Thy will be done," sucking at the cotton brought to his lips like vinegar to Christ so that we recall Christ's agony; and when the boy promises, Ledwell nods in acceptance of death. The concern with duty, with gifts (the puppy and Rosa's flowers), with the relationship between father and son, with light and dark, with a supernatural surround, and with names and faces are all constants in the fiction of Reynolds Price.

Faces are important for the clues they may offer, but often they are unreliable. Rosa searches the Phelps boy's face in vain for signs of his experience; and though she recalls Christ's statue as having "the kindest face she had ever seen" (10–11), that face is no longer visible. Faces can blur, as Wesley's identity merges briefly with that of Ledwell's son. The importance of names is indicated by Rosa's distress in having forgotten Ledwell's name, and still more by her wish that the Ledwells might have known that "Rosacoke Mustian was sorry" (42). In one sense, Rosa's gesture is perfectly correct: the anonymity of the note accompanying her flowers, like her wish not to intrude too far on the grief of others, expresses a lovely tact. Blank curiosity like Rato's is wrong; the assertion of self, feared by Rosa in her retreat from the light, can also be an ugly egotism. Rosa, who looks like an actor to Papa, must beware of placing herself too centrally in the light of someone else's drama. At the same time Rosa must not withdraw out of embarrassment, an adolescent's acute fear of exposing the self, for the Ledwells are doubly isolated by their death and by their need to face it in a strange new place. Rosa's new uncertainty, then, about the balance achieved by her gesture is admirable; and Price's use of names and faces to reveal both human solidarity and isolation expresses his own sense of the difficulties involved in a chain of love.

The story is lightened by comedy, by references to the quaint practices of Afton society: Papa shaving his chest for a womanless wedding, for instance. Snowball, a black orderly from Warren County, serves to assert the presence of the Mustian homeplace in this alien environment; but the need he feels to play darky points also to a grotesque quality in the Southernisms with which Price has embellished his first published story. We can sense here the young author's delight in the discovery of his materials and appreciate also the reach of a style that can accommodate both jokes and "rapt, ecstatic poetry."[2]

"The Warrior Princess Ozimba"

The Warrior Princess Ozimba is an old black servant, blasted by time and hard work, who in the eighth year of her retirement rocks and dozes through the pages of this brief story. Price writes that he made the story "in commemoration of [his] vanished father . . . in propitiation for [his own] forgetfulness."[3] It is a vignette celebrating Aunt Zimby and a meditation on the precarious, suddenly blazing gift of memory which passes from Ozimba to the narrator in celebration of his father. It is also an account of the relations between white and black. Mr. Ed, the narrator, has inherited from his father—"who wanted to give her presents" (45)—the obligation to bring blue tennis shoes to Ozimba on her birthday. He performs this duty reluctantly and looks for excuses to cut his annual visit short. The greater gift that Ed bears away, renewed connection to his past, reveals both the inequality and the importance for both of association between white and black people.

Ozimba's own history remains secondary to that of Ed's family, to which much of what we learn about her is connected. Her name, withheld so that it falls like a dark jewel when it comes at last, was bestowed by Ed's great-grandfather; even her birthday was fixed arbitrarily on the Fourth of July to pacify Ed's father. "She was the oldest thing any of us knew" (44), and "she took up with Uncle Ben . . . in the Year One." Ozimba's antiquity is mysterious; her family life is vague, at least to white eyes—for she never properly marries Ben, and her children "had more or less vanished" (45). Ozimba herself is frail as "a fall leaf and nearly as dry"; she is blind now, and her grasp on Ed's world is as unstable and fading as her house which would perhaps "keep out a gentle rain" (46). After recounting a tale about Ed's father, she sinks "back in her age like sleep so deep" into "wherever she was" (49). She is associated with birds and with nature generally, with the elemental surround familiar to blacks in *A Long and Happy Life*, which contains indistinct, mysterious, and sometimes dangerous energies. Honor attaches to this status, as when black children passing by greet Ozimba "just in respect as when you speak to the sea" (51), or when the sun burnishes her skin to the color of bright old pennies—making an Indian, an exotic idol of the old woman.

Only barely aware of such forces, Ed on his way to Ozimba passes two chimneys "that had belonged to Lord-knows-what" and a "sawdust pile that had swallowed Harp Hubbard at age eleven" (46). He travels, in fact, from indifference into history and mysterious nature— just as the author, physically remote in England, had painstakingly to re-create the place that could yield the father lost in two years of forgetfulness. Ed recalls thinking as a child that Ozimba "knew things she wasn't telling" (47). Now she grants him two intimate memories of Mr. Phil, to compel his son's love: one of a child stealing mulberries, and the other of a young man carrying his white dance trousers so the mud cannot damage them. Both images, significantly, place the father in nature. And she confuses Ed with Mr. Phil so that the connection can no longer be disavowed. The final image of the story returns us to Ozimba, as her voice becomes one with the "high rushing nameless notes" (52) of a flock of small birds. In a lyrical vision of the two chimneys and birds diving from the sky, her coming death is joined to Mr. Phil's—and Ed can see it, his blindness like Ozimba's seems to lift, because for a moment of love he has again become the father.

"Michael Egerton"

The style of "Michael Egerton" is imitation Hemingway, almost embarrassing. The secret embedded in its action, however, is authentic Price; and this, his first completed story, is a powerful argument for the importance of that dialectic between solitude and community which informs all his work. The first draft began with the image of a boy, "his arms extended cruciform,"[4] whom Price had known at camp. It traced Michael's decline from popularity to mock crucifixion, without suggesting a motive for the change in Michael that provokes his campmates. Michael's pain, when his mother visits the camp to introduce her new husband and to ask how Michael likes having two fathers, was subsequently invented by Price as the cause of his friend's withdrawal from communal life. It serves not as simple explanation, but to objectify a fear of betrayal which characterizes the narrator too and makes the story his.

Michael becomes a kind of double for the narrator—first more desirable, then less. When the boys meet, Michael is described as taller than the narrator, his face "old because of the bones . . . that showed through" (54–55). To look older at twelve is an advantage, although the image hints at some prematurity of suffering. Michael is in control, however. He approaches the narrator in a friendly manner, and their connection begins—sealed by the request of Michael's father that he "keep an eye on Old Mike" (55). Again some vulnerability is implied. Michael's father is a war correspondent on his way to France, a fact which hints at the precariousness of his existence and which adds to his son's glamor. But when Michael kisses his father twice in front of everybody, the narrator's surprise suggests that Michael has exposed himself unwisely. Love is dangerous, and mockery from the crowd is not its most potent threat. Symptomatic of love's danger is the fact that Michael receives only one letter from his father; Michael's father may be neglecting him or may be dead. Still, Michael continues bravely to enjoy himself, to become popular with the other boys, and to raise hopes of their cabin's winning a baseball championship.

All that collapses following his mother's visit. Michael misses the last game, and the narrator finds him alone in the bathroom "at the window with his back to me . . . tying little knots in the shade cord" (60–61). Later that evening Michael supplies his friend with a fast, agonized explanation. But the narrator fails to respond, from a sense of inadequacy perhaps, or a lack of adequate concern: "I . . . started to reach out and touch him but I didn't. I was very tired" (61). Michael withdraws from all camp activities, and the narrator observes that the boys (meaning he) "never did anything nice for him" (62). The narrator does not participate in the week's torture of Michael; neither does he intercede or offer comfort. When Michael makes a last effort at community, dressing to attend a camp function, he is tied standing upright between two bunks, "as if he was crucified" (62). The narrator returns to untie Michael, but finds he is gone. Michael has retreated to the bathroom, with its shade cord prefiguring his crucifixion. And again the narrator balks: "I started to open the door but I didn't" (63). He returns to the singing crowd.

On the face of it, the narrator's failure to reach out to Michael is simple cowardice, an adolescent's fear of being alienated (like Michael) from the mob. More significantly, he betrays Michael in order to dissociate himself from the betrayal that Michael has suffered from his parents. Price tells us in an essay about this story that the terrors of his own childhood were "experienced so intensely as to suggest a positive yearning for abandonment, betrayal." So he divides himself between Michael and the narrator, invents divorce as the cause of Michael's withdrawal, and writes "a story in which 'I' am the betrayer, conquering a fear by becoming the fear."[5] A final explanation offered in the essay connects this story to "A Chain of Love." Referring to what he had learned from his father's death some nine months before the final draft of "Michael Egerton," Price asserts that "I cannot enter the pain of another human being any more than the pain of a dog, a starling. Maybe I shouldn't try." He

suggests that "weak tries" may be a mistake, that perhaps sufferers
should be "accorded the dignity of solitude and silence."[6]

"The Anniversary"

This is the most traditionally Southern story in Price's first collection, and the only story other than "A Chain of Love" which has
a female protagonist. Here flowers are brought not to a deathbed,
but to a grave; urgent as their delivery seems, these fast-wilting
flowers come too late. Miss Lillian Carraway has missed the anniversary of Pretty Billy's death by three days, about the margin by
which she had missed out on their wedding some forty-five years
before because her virginal reserve had sent him on a fatal hunt for
warmth elsewhere. The exchange of wedding for funeral suggests a
ballad quality; and the portrait of an aged, useless spinster, the mixture
of nostalgic charm and grotesquerie, suggests its Southern flavor.
The opposed attractions of love and solitude are seen here particularly in terms of the choice between erotic love and a continuation
of the shelter that one's original family may provide. Miss Lillian
retreats from the dangers of the hunt, abandoning the hunter to find
other prey, as Rosacoke in her deer-hunting does not. The life she
has with her bachelor brother—overshadowed by their parents, like
Miss Marina's with Mr. Isaac—is shown in a harsh, but not un-
sympathetic light.

The story opens on the day of a black funeral, which Lillian has
an obligation to attend. Unlike Rosacoke, she stays away; like Rosa,
however, she then feels another pull—toward Billy's grave when she
recalls the anniversary. Her forgetfulness, like her partial blindness,
is a sign of encroaching death (as it was for Ozimba); it is also
a betrayal of Billy and a self-protection. In these early pages, where
the narrator points to all the reminders of Billy she ignores, Miss
Lillian is at home with her parents' ghosts; later, seventeen Carraway
graves overwhelm Billy's—"the one place that wasn't a Carraway"
(73). On the way to that last bastion she passes the remains of Anteus
Hill—her family mansion, struck by lightning (as Billy was by a
broken neck) before Lillian had a chance to see it " 'in person' " (70).
The anniversary of that devastation, marked by a sentimental poem
published each year in the paper, forms an ironic parallel to the
anniversary of Billy's death, also memorialized by a cloying poem
in the Carraway parlor. Both poems testify to a wish for human con-

tinuance, and to the power of God's hand to thwart that in favor of heavenly mansions and reunions. Lillian's inclination toward the Carraways, and away from Pretty Billy, is implied also in the reference to her as Pocahontas—who married and died mourning her homeland. But it is clear, for all her reluctance then and now to confront Billy, that continuance is best served by marriage. Lillian and her brother are the last Carraways. And the need she feels to tell her story to Wash, the black child who accompanies her to the graves, and who is used as the receptacle of the tale, reflects Lillian's sense that to have been chosen in marriage—however late, however uselessly—invests her with a greater dignity than utter spinsterhood could have done.

Still, Pretty Billy and Miss Lillian would have made strange bedfellows. Her lack of resourcefulness is insisted upon throughout the story. People like Nettie Pitchford, who loves and nurses Billy, are always doing things that Lillian ought to do herself. Billy's appearance on the scene does inspire Lillian to some show of vitality, but generally his liveliness is opposed to her languor, as his love of light is countered by her preference for the dark. Lillian describes Billy as " 'the nervous type' " (83); the nerves she exhibits, however, are of an opposite kind, for he wants sex while she fears it. Billy, for all his safe-seeming prettiness, is the bull in the china shop: Lillian paints china, and he is the dangerous, erotic male who breaks the skirt off a china doll. Given to touching people, although his eyes were "so deep in his head it seemed you could never come near them" (68), Pretty Billy is a Wesley figure—he even sends funny postcards. As in *A Long and Happy Life*, Price is concerned with the distance between lovers and with the failure of communication. Thus Billy works as a telegrapher and taps out messages with Lillian's fingers—risqué or romantic messages—which Lillian cannot figure out. At her fiancé's deathbed Lillian sits about four yards off and lets him die with a laugh and a moan on his lips, with his gaze on Nettie.

We are never told straight out what Billy was hunting on the night of his death. But we know that Lillian's fear, or her distaste for intimacy, had led him to find solace and pleasure elsewhere. What Billy needed is imaged as it was for Wesley by the water Nettie uses to wipe his brow; after death his hand (which Lillian cannot touch) is "curled inwards to make a cup like a sea shell waiting for water" (89). " 'Give her something she wants' " (87), Billy says; and Nettie comes later to claim his gold ring, which Lillian's father

48   REYNOLDS PRICE

impedes since it would be an emblem of her true connection to Billy.
Lillian does not break down at Billy's death, as " 'any woman should' "
(88). Preserving an untarnished image of Billy, she protects herself—
how thoroughly we cannot know, though Lillian is " 'a mighty good
forgetter' " (90)—from the truth which strikes like lightning on
Anteus Hill at the story's close. Light associated with Billy flashes
on her roof's spilled silver paint, and Lillian's coldness melts like
"some proud mountain yielding the sun its flanks of snow" (92).
Too late, however beautifully, this aged Leda acknowledges erotic
power and is chastened, like Idle Carraway, for her pride.

"Troubled Sleep"

In "Troubled Sleep" Price continues his study of the desirable
young male whose approaches and withdrawals cause such difficulty
for the protagonist. Falcon Rodwell, loved by his cousin Edward, is
in that sense like Wesley or Michael Egerton or Pretty Billy. Each
of these characters has to some degree a visionary quality and an aura
of success; something about his completeness, his unseen self, suggests
the risk of betrayal or self-annihilation for the protagonist. An erotic
component in the relationship between the two young boys, not
evident in "Michael Egerton," is striking here—so that it is easy, for
instance, to hear Rosacoke's voice when Edward thinks of confronting
Falc's careless indifference, "making up hurt questions . . . such as
'Falcon Rodwell, why in the world—if you are going to be my
cousin and spend every summer with me and take what I give—do
you do things like tonight?' " (98). Direct questioning of this sort
fails with Falc, as it does with Wesley: "you'd be in silence up to
your ears" (98). Still, " 'Help,' " the story's first word, is what Falc
claims to offer as he approaches the Dark Ring—a woodland clearing,
"snakes knee-deep surely on all sides" (93), which the boys use "for
burying things and ceremonies" (94). And this recalls the broomstraw ring of *A Long and Happy Life*, as well as Price's wish "to clear
and tend and fortify a circle in the forest, then to stage games there."[7]

Edward relates the events of a single evening when his father
sends him to bed for calling Falc a cheater, and he escapes to the
Dark Ring, "thinking of nothing but ways to pay them back and win
them back" (94). The sense of injustice pains him less than his
isolation. While Edward resents Falc's independence, he is also deeply
attracted to it, as by the "lighthouse" Falc is said to resemble. Falc

appears as an almost visionary source of light, with the tails of lightning bugs stuck to his forehead; that light recalls Wesley's, as Falc's name recalls Wesley's link to the hawk, and as both boys are closely associated with the natural surround. As Falc enters the Ring his arms change color "the way a crow's wings will . . . leaving you glad you noticed him" (96). Yet Falc has come "for reasons of his own that he might never tell" (95) and "not by the one right ceremonial way," but like a free agent, "breaking every rule" (96). Falc is all Edward has, he thinks—forgetting his father and that he does not really have either one. He waits for touch or speech, and touch fails because Falc is not thinking "on similar lines" (98).

Speech comes first from Falc, who asks " 'Where do you wish we were?' " Edward answers " 'Dead' . . . the thing I had to say to start his game and the thing I meant, this night" (99). Amusing and ghoulish, Falc's answer is a long soaring flight of fantasy in which he is besieged by all manner of adversity, succumbing only to germs, the one thing he cannot see. His story casts Edward in a minor, almost female role: neither as the widow who would throw herself on a funeral pyre nor as a co-adventurer is Edward allowed to follow, and he is left feeling "worse than ever" (102). Falc's taste for a dangerous, unseen world, suggested also by his wish to see the crazy lady who plays an invisible organ, implies the two risks entailed by Edward's love—that Falc will die, or simply that he will pass out of view.

Desperately reaching for some commitment, Edward insists that they " 'die in real life' " (102). He rejects any proposals that might end with Falc's surviving when he does not, and they settle at last on exposure to deadly lunar rays—insanity, provided that it comes to both alike, will be proof enough. Besides, it will be embarrassing to Edward's parents and "pay them back." The boys strip to the waist and lie like "two narrow boats left together in a silent bloodless world" (106)—recalling how Falc had refused to become Edward's Blood Brother. When Edward thinks Falc has died, he tries to follow in imagination, but envisions only a place where Falc will be surrounded by other adoring boys and impervious to Edward—a misery which sends him into sleep at last. That waking dream has shown Edward the ultimate separateness of his life, and "*knowing* that for the first time" (108), he is able to accept a compromise. When Falc thinks Edward is dead and shows a ceremonial sadness, Edward is soothed. He waits until Falc is asleep and places an arm on his chest—

although earlier he would not, since "Falc had never been too strong
on touching people" (107). Edward takes what he can, for as long
as he can. The story closes with a shift in point of view, acceptable
because it brings the third important player into the Dark Ring, as
Edward's father comes and finds them sleeping "in each other's arms
at least and breathing slow" (109).

"Uncle Grant"

Perhaps the most nearly perfect story in the collection is "Uncle
Grant." Its most striking feature is a sense of unrelenting, brutal accuracy in the assessment of how far Reynolds Price and his family
lived up to their responsibilities toward Grant Terry, their black
yardman. Price allows for every sign of care and duty, but he does
not shrink by a hair's breadth from any of the failures toward Grant
or from recording those inequalities based on race that he knows
must weigh against him. He writes with the conviction that such
errors count, but that love can survive them—and that he can prove
it by his steady gaze. An early example of that gaze is the long
sentence that shows in exact detail how Grant would receive the
news that Reynolds, way off in Oxford, England, had been thinking
of him for a whole week. Thus he asserts the power of memory and
imagination to raise Grant from the dead—literally dead, Grant had
also been long absent from the author's mind. So the story, in which
Reynolds recalls having assured Grant that he would meet his friends
again in heaven, gives proof not only of his right to claim immor-
tality on Grant's behalf, but also of his long-delayed willingness to
" 'step out yonder and speak' " (128) to Uncle Grant, as his father
had requested. Price meets him on the other side of racial barriers,
transcending those and the grave and his own shameful indifference.

As with Ozimba, Grant's age and origins are shrouded in mystery.
His name also descends from a warrior associated with black history,
since probably he was "named for a general his parents heard of
who set them free" (113). As the children pretended that Ozimba
was an Indian, so Reynolds admired Grant for being three parts
Indian; and when Grant finds an arrowhead or saves Reynolds from
a blacksnake, he becomes "a fearless hero to imitate" instead of a
tame "nurse" (118). That wish to mythologize the American black
into some apparently more noble history, either Indian or African,

takes another turn in the postcard of Akhnaton that Reynolds buys in England and then decides is " 'the one picture left of Uncle Grant' " (113). His week's recollection is triggered by this likeness of the Egyptian pharaoh who converted his people to the worship of "the one true god, the streaming disc, the sun" (113). And again, as with Ozimba, the black servant becomes a radiant figure for the natural word that had begun to recede for the narrator: Grant's special gift, like that of Akhnaton's god, is that he could " 'make things grow' " (115).

Uncle Grant is essentially a solitary man. His wife and child have been left behind, and the only connection he has to another black person occurs when he falls "in some sort of love with a girl named Katie" (123). Like the bond to Will Price, that phrase—"some sort of love"—suggests the value of undefined relationships, those which transcend the usual categories of attachment. Reynolds recalls how his father had fulfilled his obligations to Grant (when he could) almost as one would court a lover, careful not to offend. "Nobody knows why they sat there night after night," talking—"unless they loved each other" (117). After Will's death, Grant never again mentions his name; with intense, quiet determination he leaves if conversation turns in that direction.

Reynolds's own connection to Grant began to fail in adolescence. His final, Christmas visit to Grant in the Welfare Home was made only because Reynolds's aunt reminded him that " 'nobody God made will appreciate it more' " (132). It turns out that Grant has been waiting for him. Though the Price family's gifts of chewing tobacco and bedroom shoes (recalling Ozimba's tennis shoes) are useless now, this visit matters. Reynolds chats a while, tells Grant that he can get into heaven without baptism, and leaves "thinking gradually of my own business, not thinking of him . . . feeling I had no reasons" (136). But the story gives those reasons. It closes with a precise accounting of what honors were bestowed or withheld in the matter of Grant's funeral; with a long penultimate sentence which elegiacally repeats facts given at the start; and with the claim that Grant's "final joke, if it *was* a joke (him saying he would see me in Heaven), whoever it was on, it was not on him." "This is the point" (137), Price tells us, of the whole story. All the old family jokes he has told on Grant cannot diminish that fearless hero's dignity. In heaven they will meet as promised.

"The Names and Faces of Heroes"

The title story of the collection reiterates images and themes from the preceding stories and serves as a resolution to the whole. The narrator is a young boy whose fear of bed-wetting and homesickness at camp, for instance, as in "Michael Egerton," or whose admiration for Tarzan, as in "Troubled Sleep," suggests that one protagonist has appeared with various names and faces almost throughout the book. Those details reveal also the kind of boy he is: deeply, fearfully attached to his parents, yearning to be stronger and braver than he is. In "Ozimba" and "Uncle Grant" he is older and so more distant, until the maelstrom of reminiscence returns him to childhood; here a vision of the future allows the protagonist to appear at both ages, as memory does in "Uncle Grant." Preacher was one of his father's names for Reynolds; Preacher's father, like Ledwell in "A Chain of Love," dies of lung cancer and is linked to Christ; Uncle Grant appears also, under the name of Uncle Hawk. But the important autobiographical detail, surfacing both here and in "Troubled Sleep," is the father's promise that he will change his life, will give up drink, if God will save his wife and son from death in childbed.

In the first sentence Preacher expresses a central fear: " 'We are people in love. . . . What our enemies want is to separate us. Will we end together? Will we end alive?' " (138). Preacher and his father are mystically isolated and joined in a car at night, driving home from a trip to Raleigh where they have heard a sermon delivered by a man who saw Christ. The phrase "people in love" takes on something of its usual erotic meaning from the emphasis given to Preacher's position in the car. His head rests on his father's lap, on his genitals—of which the child is powerfully, insistently aware.

The two principal themes of the story, the boy's anxious love for his father and his fear of approaching manhood, converge on the issue of the "lacks" which he hopes to control by finding a hero. His "enemies" can be fought, Preacher thinks, his manhood can be safely achieved, if he can find a hero who has what he lacks. But he has trouble finding his "*mortal* foe" (142), since so many faults—selfishness, envy, pride, dishonesty, distrust of his parents—are apparent to him. His list supplies the portrait of a boy who values himself highly and does not receive sufficient acknowledgment of who and what he is—which is different from what other boys are, for good and ill. That sense of difference makes Preacher blame himself as well, makes him yearn to be like those other boys who play ball so easily and well; he is unsure how far to be pleased with the gifts he has, for singing and drawing. Preacher reveals how his father had quickly despaired of teaching him to play baseball, which he had loved and which Preacher must learn if he is not to be mocked by the other boys; and later he observes that his father stares straight ahead "as if through snow he watched boys playing skillful games with natural grace" (177). That sense of difference is also the explanation of his childhood's "darkest fear that I am not the blood child of Jeff and Rhew McCraw, that I was adopted at birth, that someday a strange man will come and rightfully claim me" (149). His fear of separation from the father first takes that form, then becomes a fear of rejection by the father for what he is, and finally is a fear of death (which is his father's main fear, too).

In his search for a hero Preacher rejects the famous dead, finding in each case some abuse of power, some cruelty toward dependents. Believing that " 'a man makes his face' " (140), Preacher looks first to the candidate's face and then to his deeds. He wants a hero to look like a hero, as if he can change people's lives; Preacher dislikes those portraits of Christ that seem too mild or effeminate. He assumes that Mr. Barden should not be his father's hero because he is too skinny, and he has rejected various uncles out of hand for being too fat. Other uncles are "liable at any time to start drinking and disappear" (145); like the famous dead, and perhaps like Preacher's father, these buccaneer uncles abuse the love that they compel. As a last resort, Preacher considers his father. His face is a problem mainly because it changes when he "mocks" people; this disturbs Preacher, just as the multiplicity of Christ's faces does, because he wants the chameleon pinned down, reliable as a source of love and a guide for his own life. Only the father's wrist seems heroic, indeed seems "grander . . . than he needs or deserves." Feeling his father's pulse, angry at his "distances" and implied rejection of Preacher, the boy senses his own growing power, the possibility of independence: "poor as I am at games and play, I could press in now" (159) and kill. Later, on that same wrist, Preacher will trace proudly his own name, as lovers do on trees.

Christ's failure to show his face to Preacher's father seems to the child a betrayal and reflects his own passionate need for the father's constancy. As the hero of a thousand faces, the father is clearly linked to Christ—by the wound in his hand, by the beauty Preacher had

"planned for Jesus" (172) and sees on his father's face when he
returns to the car after a frightening absence, and by "the letter J
perfect" (174) which marks his chest in the death vision. Since
" 'Jesus is the one that did not die' " (160), Preacher thinks he would
be an appropriate hero for a man afraid of death. But his father
chooses someone closer to home, the man who helped him to keep his
promise. It seems that his father's mortal foe is not death itself, but
that inclination—of which drink is only an agent—to turn his face
away from those who need him. A model of constancy was provided
by Mr. Barden, who was always there when Jeff McCraw needed
him. The lack of constancy in his father makes Preacher reject him
as hero—until he recognizes that his father did change his life. His
constancy was imperfect and hard-won, but at his father's deathbed
Preacher vows to " 'turn in my tracks on myself my foe with you as
shield' " (176). What Preacher learns from his father, or tries to
learn, is not to ask too much and to acknowledge plentiful receipts.
In choosing his father as shield, moreover, Preacher acknowledges his
own foe: a self-destructive tendency to turn away from the exchange
of sustenance with those he loves.

The vision of his father's death begins when Preacher eases himself into sleep by cupping his own boyish groin, as his father had
done briefly before. A circle of light appears around that groin, which
is now an adult's—first his own, and then mysteriously his father's.
The light expands to reveal a hospital bed, his father's coming death.
Preacher maintains his grip, fearing that "our skin has joined maybe
past parting." He wishes to release his father for both their sakes, to
leave each whole; he also, probably, would prefer that his father not
be aware of Preacher's intimate touch. But as he tries to remove his
hand, his father's penis rises as if Preacher had "given love not pain."
He calls on Jesus to effect their mutual release, " 'I do not ask to see
Your face but come in *some* shape now' "—and again He comes in
the shape of Preacher's father, as a "shudder begins beneath my hand
in his core our core" (175), the beginning of a death spasm which
causes his father's head to roll toward Preacher, perhaps to witness
Preacher's hold. With his free hand the son feels his father's wrist
and discovers that the pulse has stopped. The pardon that Preacher
asks, for his excessive demands upon the father, for his past lacks, or
perhaps for what he may feel is an unnatural love, seems to have
been granted. And Preacher's hands are freed as the vision fades. The
story ends with the boy looking forward both to the time when he

will begin work on that promise to change his life, and also to the
years remaining before "they" (the enemies without and within)
will separate him from Jeff McCraw.

Chapter Four
A Generous Man
Plot Summary and Introduction

Price's second novel is another chapter in the Mustian family history. It begins on the morning after Milo's sexual initiation by Lois Provo, who has come to Warrenton with her aunt Selma (really her mother) and their traveling snake show. When Rato's dog Phillip is diagnosed as mad, Rato and Phillip and a python called Death escape to the woods, pursued by Milo and a posse led by Rooster Pomeroy. Milo leaves the hunt to recover from his first bout of drunkenness, to make love to the impotent Rooster's wife Kate, and to hear her tale of a boy whom Milo mysteriously resembles. The Provo and Pomeroy plots converge at this point, for Milo had reminded Selma of the same elusive Tommy Ryden, who was kin to Milo and father to Lois. Tommy's ghost returns to lead Milo to the insurance money meant for Lois, Death is killed, Selma reveals her maternity, Milo and Lois make love, and Rato and the dog come safely home.

The novel began, Price tells us in "News for the Mineshaft: An Afterword to *A Generous Man*,"[1] when its author sought relief in a troubled time. He was "beached" by John Kennedy's murder, a loss which chimed with the dark matter of a novel he had begun, in which he had "personal stakes" (*The Surface of Earth*). So he turned to two separate, remembered tales of "a runaway circus-snake and a mad dog whose rural owners set it free to rave" (*NM*, 72), deciding that he could yoke these to the Mustian family in a kind of farce. He took pleasure in the new book's movement and language, in the creation of a past for characters whose futures he had long since fixed, and in the "guying of as many as possible of the sacred solemnities of Southern fiction, [his] own included" (*NM*, 73).

But by the time he had changed the working title from *A Mad Dog and a Boa Constrictor* to *Clear Day*, the novel's dark theme had begun to surface: "the theme was *loss*" (*NM*, 74). Price traces then the major occurrences of the phrase "clear day" and lays bare in that process the frightening skeleton of the book. The story is Milo's, "as he reaches (in three days) the height of his manhood, poises in clear

56

broad day, descends" (*NM*, 79–80). Although the novel lifts Milo, as it did his author, into a sense of fun and new possibility, it describes only a brief intermission, a prelude to the experience of loss and tragedy of a diminished life. The last bone of the skeleton rattles into place with the concluding sentence of the novel: "It was morning (clear, cloudless, the oldest gift), would be morning oh six hours yet."[2] Six hours is a short time, given what Price refers to as "Donne's use of the same metaphor—'His first minute, after noon, is night' " (*NM*, 80). Thus, the titular optimism of *Clear Day* is subtly, dangerously overcast, an effect which applies also to *A Generous Man*— the title which Price selected when he found that the other had been preempted. The Milo we know from *A Long and Happy Life* has lost the pleasure of generosity. He is an embittered man who does exactly what he had prophesied as the alternative to flight at the end of *A Generous Man*: " 'What I won't do, *can't* do is stand in my tracks—my ancestors' tracks—and be whipped dry, dead but can't lie down for sixty more years' " (272). Minutes later, he is fixed in those tracks for good. Milo's day is over.

Price suggests that *A Generous Man* is not actually a novel because its story—replete with ghosts, prophecy, and so on—is "miraculous" in form. It suspends both the laws of the realistic novel and those physical laws that we rely on to shield us from "the large world—that terrible, perhaps even benevolent world which turns, huge, around and beneath our neater world which agrees to forbid it. The dead, incompletions, the past which is future" (*NM*, 85). That statement reveals, of course, the author's belief in a supernatural reality and the possibility of our altering the decision to ignore it. It implies also that the realistic novel might be redefined when those laws change, as laws do. In his scholarly voice, however, Price considers whether his book should instead be termed a romance.

He cites several definitions of that genre—"in which stylized characters capable of allegorical expansion move through 'strange adventures, separations, wanderings across seas and lands, rescues miraculously effected, dangers overcome and trials passed, until the final triumph of reunion with loved relatives.' " That definition succeeds well enough for *A Generous Man*, as Price suggests, but for the last thirty pages; there it falters, since "surely the minimal requirement for romance is a happy ending" (*NM*, 82). In fact, if Price had speeded up the homecoming of Rato and Phillip, he might have ended the book with Part Two and satisfied that requirement. The last thirty pages form a dark coda, almost another ending which comes when the action of the romance is over. Just as Price's attention to "the large world" means that his novel will encroach upon territories normally excluded by that realistic genre, so his darker, realistic vision means that the "wish-fulfillment" which is the basic "strategy" of romance must be subverted. The "romance" ending is followed by the realistic, unhappy ending of Part Three, and then perhaps by an implicit comic resolution in the hereafter (outside the limits of the book) which obtains for any significantly Christian work. Reunions are accomplished, foiled, and by that last projection won again. Thus the romance of *A Generous Man* prefigures a Christian resolution (which is implied by all of Price's work) and exists in a dialectical relationship with its realistic tendency. That relationship is also roughly parallel to the interplay of comedy and tragedy.

Price makes the interesting assertion that romance is concerned with arousing and at least partially allaying "our oldest fears—that we are not the children of our parents, that lovers may be permanently parted, that nature is indifferent if not hostile." These clearly are Price's own central fears. Because *A Generous Man* moved beyond its first, partial easing of those fears, to "renunciations, further (and final) separations, a grim future seen, a grim present faced" (*NM*, 83), he is prepared to deny it the label of romance. Northrup Frye, however, allows a more pessimistic definition of the genre: "The romancer deals with individuality, with characters *in vacuo* idealized by revery, and ... something nihilistic and untamable is likely to keep breaking out of his pages."[3] That phenomenon occurs in *A Generous Man*. As characters depart the mind-dulling borders of an everyday social reality, they release not only their ideal selves, but also their darkest knowledge of a reality that opposes the ideal. The return to everyday responsibilities will entail for Milo in particular not the incorporation of his ideal self, but its destruction. By the time of *A Long and Happy Life* he is nearly indistinguishable from the sorts of men who comprise Rooster's posse.

Just as the genre of the work hovers somewhere between the romance and the realistic novel, so its language is an amalgam of the artificial and the natural. The success of *A Generous Man* for any given reader will depend on how well he thinks that mixture has been achieved. Price remarks upon "the conversion of mid-South farm-dialect into forms and meters which appear, I think, natural but are thoroughly made from the inside by pleasure" (*NM*, 73). An element of game-playing is also apparent in the claim that one of his sentences employs "the meter of the *William Tell* Overture" (*NM*, 74), or that certain scenes have a formal resemblance to scenes in operas by Rossini and Verdi. It is not clear from "News for the Mineshaft" whether Price believes that such playfulness may coexist with language that is "the literally reflexive response of all my available faculties to the moment at hand." But that definition of his style as simple accuracy, fidelity to vision, is an article of faith for Reynolds Price. He resists passionately any suggestion of "manner" or "appliqué of decoration" (*NM*, 87). Readers who expect that "manner" begins where naturalistic dialogue leaves off may be confused by the author's definition of his style. Fidelity in language, however, is aimed at something larger than what a machine for recording voices might contain, for "the moment at hand" is always imaginative.

The characters speak differently from the folk of a literal Afton, although their speech is modeled on an existing dialect. Sometimes, we may feel, they speak too differently—as when Lois describes Selma's sliding " 'in and out of some speechless grief the way normal people change a suit of clothes' " (34). The author's own characteristic diction and phrasing are everywhere apparent, and occasionally the author's voice is heard so strongly that his characters are momentarily effaced.

The dominant effect, however, is to unify the characters, casting the spell of a single vision over their lives. This unification by language parallels the operation of coincidence in the plot, as both work to create the impression of a privileged time—an interval in which the usually alien, diverse strands of human (as well as animal and supernatural) life have miraculously come together. Thus, when Selma tries to save her snake from Rato's dog, who moves like a "drunk," she breaks into "a run more crippled than even the worst of Phillip's (she suffered rheumatism)" (62), and we recall more or less consciously two previous interlocking descriptions: Phillip, according to Milo, has " 'rheumatism—or something similiar' " (14), and Dr. Fuller, weaving drunkenly, looks like a snake to Phillip. In a purely realistic novel such links might appear too calculated; here, they contribute to the sense of holiday which informs romance.

One of the most remarkable features of *A Generous Man* is the precision of direction it gives particularly to physical movement. As Price remarks, the action is "balletic and clear-lined" (*NM*, 73). For the sake of accuracy, much of this description is extremely complex; we may feel it is too laborious, as in the description of Milo balancing on Dr. Fuller's fence. But Price has refused "to contract with readers-on-horseback, racing by" (*NM*, 86). We cannot know what he thinks, Price warns, until we see—the "crucial verb is *see*" (*NM*, 70)—what he says.

Milo and Rosacoke (Part One)

The novel opens with Milo's name, as his mother calls to wake him. Price makes clear immediately that this is not an ordinary day and that it belongs to Milo. His door is closed, and he is dreaming "like money smuggled into his head" (3) of Lois—of his new sexual knowledge, which he hoards, which the metaphor suggests is valuable and illicit in the family context. Two conflicts are implied: the opposition of family and eroticism (which is inevitable with growth, and inevitably selfish to some degree), and the further question of how Milo will deal with his burgeoning sexuality as it affects his partners. On both fronts the novel will test Milo's generosity, his ability to cope with the demands of an insurgent self and the needs of others. Neither the closed door nor the act of dreaming is usual for Milo, and Rosa enters without knocking to rouse Milo for family duties.

What she confronts is Milo naked, stripped for the business of his dream, his new life. Still ignorant that Milo is aimed elsewhere, she responds with delight—an innocent, half-sexual playfulness. Rosa announces that Milo must go with the family to the veterinarian since Phillip is sick, and Milo asserts his new independence, a belief in free will which becomes one of the central issues of the book: " 'I hadn't got to do nothing but die' " (4). When Rosa places a hand "sudden on his butt" (5), Milo responds by standing up in the bed, poised for flight in a tableau which echoes through the novel like Wesley in his pecan tree. He looks out the window, regretting leaves which obscure his vision of the ferris wheel, five miles off, where Lois is—too far for the naked eye, as Rosa points out. As in *A Long and Happy Life*, Rosacoke is left behind while the visionary, sexual male stares into his future. The narrator observes that these leaves are six weeks away from death, an interval which seems excessive to Milo in his eagerness for sight of Lois, but which anticipates the six brief hours left of morning at the novel's end. Milo is right to hurry, to use what time he has. The irony, however, is that Milo's day will be over when it has scarcely begun: like the ferris wheel, he will rise toward the pinnacle and instantly descend. The sense of diurnal journey, where the day becomes the life, is enforced by Price's decision to begin each of the novel's three sections with Milo waking, to end the first two (and so, implicitly, the third) with his fall into sleep—the harbinger of death.

For the moment, however, Milo's day seems glorious. On his hands before Rosa, rejoicing in the knowledge that separates them, Milo speaks boastfully, cryptically of exercising the snake with Lois again that night. By this time Milo is wearing Rato's underpants—an ironic version of the token which a lady bestows on her knight, for Milo wears these throughout his adventures. In his role as knight, Milo responds to Rosa's urging with a spirited battlecry: " 'On to save Rato, spare him pain, return him to his rightful place in his home!' " (7). These words are prophetic, a sign that some external force is already at work in Milo, for Rato is not yet missing; further, they imply the real objects of a quest in which Milo will learn to be merciful and will restore Rooster to his rightful place with Kate.

Like Wesley in *A Long and Happy Life*, Milo is the youthful knight whose purpose is to restore fertility in a kingdom ruled by an aging Fisher King. Within his family, this pattern is implied by our first sight of Papa, staring impotently at the fields "as if staring might revive, make grow, harvest" (7). It accounts for the insistence throughout the novel on the family's need for Milo as Papa's successor and for the odd insistence on Papa's courtly relationship to Lois. The sexual innuendo about Lois and Papa, like the many allusions to Rooster's impotence, establishes Milo as the youthful male who performs what the older man cannot. But Milo does not rudely dispossess the Fisher King: in the hallowed interval of Milo's day, Papa enjoys almost supernaturally renewed vitality, while the sheriff's profit extends to " 'the new Apple King!' " (261) whom Kate will bear.

Rosa is excluded at the breakfast table from the sexual talk which joins Milo and Papa. The hints that began in Milo's bedroom continue, and Rosacoke's pain at being locked away from Milo in childhood increases; it becomes in fact a dominant theme in this first part of the novel, a dark counterpoint to the gaiety of Milo and a forewarning of woman's misery. The discussion of Puss Ellis, the town whore, and of the hootchy-kootchy show, where Macey's glasses disappear into the first of the novel's many vaginal abysses, suggests another difficulty in the way of Milo's libido. Such bawdiness verges on dirt, and the sexual camaraderie of men tends to aim that dirt at women—as we see more clearly during the hunt.

Milo begins his day with confidence inspired by the night before, telling Phillip to smile—" 'Milo's on duty. You're half-cured already' " (7). That faith waivers as the Mustians pass the carnival on their way to town, and Milo sees it shrunken, deflated in natural light. He determines to waste " 'no money there tonight,' " until he sees Lois waving "as if she were captive and pled for rescue" (17–18). His mistake had been to think of his goal in terms of mere self-interest, which diminishes its value; the magic of Milo's quest is dependent upon his generosity, which (physically, it seems) lifts him and the environment in which he moves. Waiting for Lois in town, Milo stations himself on the veterinarian's fence—balancing there, floating above the ordinary, wishing for sight of Lois as he had done while standing on his bed at home. Again he is " 'aimed away' " (29) from the sister who tries to find shelter even in the shadow Milo casts. That shadow, however, suggests that time has taken Milo from Rosa—not, as Rosa thinks, some wish "to hurt her" (30). She sings the only song that Milo knows, hoping that he will answer as usual with a chorus of "Fare Thee Well." But Milo is concerned only with greeting Lois when she comes; she approaches, and he beckons "inwards to himself" (31), where Rosa wants to be.

Although opposed to one another here, as the desired and the rejected woman, Lois and Rosa are equally types of the female to whom the buccaneer male causes pain. When Milo does blithely sing his song, Lois will feel abused that he has not offered speech instead; merely sexual interest seems to Lois, as it does to Rosacoke, an insult. Price is clearly sympathetic to both girls, but he is also supportive of the male whose spirits sink when women expect too much, suffer and refuse to name their woes. For much of the novel an energy which seems to flow from Milo keeps the action and characters united and several inches off the ground. But the threat of disunity, of descent into isolation, is always present; and it is caused in part by the clash of an excessive sensitivity in women and a paucity of the same in men.

Although Milo is generally insensitive to Rosa in this first section of the novel and resentful of "her hold, her try on his life" (18), he does once attempt to soothe her. He begins by claiming that Lois " 'is nothing to me,' " and means to explain his interest by revealing the sexual nature of their encounter. Instead he offers a lie "told to shield her from his own growing, as if his life, his sudden needs and powers, were a rising light that could stunt, sear" (19–20). Rosa also wishes to protect him from knowledge which "she would always have to ignore to live her life" (18). Presumably, her unwelcome news relates to the essential isolation of human beings, their frequent inability to answer one another's needs. She sees Milo moving away from her and fears for him as well as for herself. The sexual knowledge from which he tries to protect Rosa would not allay those fears, for isolation in that sphere (as Rosa will learn from Wesley) is not uncommon and can be more devastating than any other.

Late that evening, returning from his first pursuit of Death, Rato, and Phillip, Milo finds Rosa sharing his bed and Lois in his sister's room next door. This arrangement dramatizes Milo's old connection to Rosa and his wish to exchange one girl for the other. Rosa has been dreaming of Milo standing "in the fork of a tree high above her" (67) and spreading his arms to jump. The image of Wesley in the pecan tree is obviously recalled and forecast, and the "fork," since that word is used consistently to describe the fork of a woman's legs, suggests that sex will be Milo's downfall or his point of departure. In the dream she cries " 'You will die and ruin us, Milo,' " and he replies " 'I am almost a man. I must fall to rise.' " He jumps, "rising not falling as he had foretold," and Rosa's last image is of Milo still floating with "no thought of when that day might end" (67). Although Milo must fall into sexuality in order to rise as a man, his day (his ascension) will end in time and sooner than he thinks. Rosa awakes, and they exchange news. Milo says of the hunt that " 'What is to be will be,' " and Rosa echoes that; she looks forward to a " 'terrible future,' " wishing nonetheless that her " 'time' " (72) would come quickly. The shared fatalism of male and female differs stereotypically, for Rosa's vision is of a future spent yearning for the male, while Milo's fear is that his wish for successful action (the earning of various prizes) will not be met. The last image of this section, where Milo stands rejected by Lois at her door, suggests an obstacle to Milo's expansive will. He is humiliated but able to forget it. Rosa, however, who imagines the scene with perfect accuracy, as if she "had entered him ghostly" (77), will not forget. It becomes for her a permanent truth, a revelation of the barrier between male and female.

The Hunt (Part Two)

The hunt begins at noon on the day following Rato's flight. Papa
and Lois have formed a search party of their own, leaving Milo to
join the sheriff and his posse. Although Milo's spirits are revived by
anticipation of the hunt, he is less secure than on the previous morning. Lois has delivered him some curt rebuffs, culminating in the
refusal to admit him to her bed; and those experiences signal Milo's
need for an improved understanding of the sexuality with which he
is invested like "a rising light that could stunt, sear" (20) or hallow
his day. The first stage in Milo's progress toward a mature sexual
understanding is the encounter with Rooster Pomeroy. Like Papa,
and like Dr. Fuller, the veterinarian who is an embittered victim of
old age and loneliness, Rooster represents exhaustion; in his case,
the ability to perform sexually has failed. Rooster notices Milo's resemblance to Tom Ryden, his wife's lost love, and recognizes too
Milo's dawning virility. He seizes, therefore, an opportunity to secure
the future of his name and marriage, and offers Milo this advice:
" 'Use what the good Lord give you *now*, and use it every chance the
day provides' " (86). We assume that Rooster guides Milo toward
Kate with subliminally acknowledged purpose, inspired by the magic
of Milo's day. Rooster's advice has a corollary, however, which is not
given Milo until his part in the hunt is finished: " 'Don't step too
high,' " avoid " 'flinging dirt' " (140) on yourself and others.

For Milo and for Rooster, who calls this job " 'the *height* of my
life,' " and for all the posse, the hunt offers a means of ending
" 'bigger men in the eyes of their loved ones and enemies' " (108).
They seek to ease various humiliations, particularly at the hands of
women, by proving themselves in an heroic enterprise. Similarly,
Phillip and Death seek to restore their "ruined pride" (65) by escaping into the wilderness from a threatening domesticity. The masculinity of Death is insisted upon by a multitude of phallic jokes, and
Phillip also is linked to the tradition of the vagabond male by Milo's
claim that he is part " 'traveling salesman' " (7). Animals and men
alike rejoice in the prospect of a worthy foe. As frequently occurs in
romantic accounts of battles and quests, however, more energy is devoted to oratory than to action. The preamble is lengthy, involving
a mock-epic list of the participants, an embellishment of Death's
stature as the chief adversary, and a recitation of prayers for the
return of lost things. Only the women, who serve ham biscuits to the

departing questers, seem particularly concerned with the hunt's literal purpose. Rosacoke, whose role in the novel is nearly finished at this point, wishes also that Milo would come " *'back* in his old right mind.' " But Milo is determined to forge on, to finish the day by taking his " 'ease on some girl' " (110), and the sexual dimension of Milo's quest will receive considerably more attention than his efforts to find the snake, the dog, and the boy.

Armed with Rooster's first piece of advice, Milo soon finds himself in an environment where its corollary is sorely needed. Yancey Breedlove, the sheriff's deputy, is newly married and reeks of a sexual bravado which Rooster explains as an attempt to assuage his ruined pride. Like most men in Rooster's view, Yancey finds himself baffled and caught by the woman he took to be his worthy prey. Milo equates Yancey's situation with that of his own dead father, whose misery and drunkenness derived from a sense of imprisonment. Milo had begun the hunt with a prayer asking help " 'to live with whatever we find' " (109), but Yancey has not found the grace to do so. Rather like Milo in *A Long and Happy Life*, Yancey inflates and cheapens the satisfaction of his marriage bed—unleashing the worst of his hostility on the black girl they meet in the woods. Buck's story of his involvement with Della, intended to praise the utility of black women, is another example of the ugly phallicism that is rampant among Rooster's men. Even the virginal Macey, aping his disappointed elders, flings dirt in the general direction of womankind.

Milo's response to all of this is problematic, although perhaps less so than Rooster's. The author's own stance may also be unclear. Racism, for instance, is not criticized overtly; but Milo and Rooster prove themselves more capable than the rest of perceiving the black girl and boy as human beings and act to help them. That circumstance together with the sheer ugliness of this posse's behavior to the blacks may seem to Price sufficient judgment. More distinctly than its racism, however, the phallic preoccupations of the posse are clearly shared by Rooster and Milo—who begins the hunt with measuring his "forward growth" (101). That celebration is seen by Price as natural and inoffensive, different in kind from the angry and compensatory phallicism of Yancey. When Yancey offers to purchase the black girl for Milo's use and Macey's, Milo declines. And Rooster approves his decision. He proceeds to outline, however, an apology for the male species. The level of tolerance he displays, arguing in defense of a hypothetical rapist that " 'maybe that gal just needed that humping to calm her nerves' " (130), is obviously excessive.

Whereas Rooster approves of turning a blind eye to human frailty, Milo's eyes absorb like "heavy magnets" each sight displayed for his "gradual merciless judgment" (135). Provoked by the liquor he has consumed, and by the hysterical dance of the moonshiner's boy, Milo intervenes to protect him and to denounce the " 'sorry lives' " of Rooster and the others, " 'the mess they have made on other people.' " Milo's phrase anticipates the sheriff's injunction against flinging dirt, and Rooster chooses this moment to deliver that second piece of advice. On one level, the sheriff's advice is well-timed. Milo does fling dirt upon himself and others: his judgment is abusive, as when he elaborates crudely upon Rooster's impotence, and he is covered with vomit, like the drunken father whose model he had wished to escape. He participates in the filthy talk which he criticizes in the others so that Price can reveal a vital source of Milo's disgust: with reason, Milo fears his own descent into meanness and an embittered captivity. He is appalled at being asked " 'to think the world's like this' " (139). Still Milo's judgment is more admirable than the defense of a lower life which is implied by Rooster's command to " 'keep your feet to the ground' " (140). That advice is good so far as it refers to kindness or a check on rampant sexuality, but wrong to the extent that it denies the possibility of judgment or Milo's aspiration toward a higher level of existence. Drunkenness renders Milo incapable for now of continuing the hunt, and he is sent by Rooster with the moonshine to where Kate is waiting.

Milo, Tom, and Kate (Part Two)

The first major exposition of the Ryden subplot through Kate is preceded by numerous clues, beginning with Milo's description to Rosa of how Selma Provo had watched him " 'like something hurtful, a hawk in a henhouse' " (19). Tommy Ryden enters the story by name when the Mustians encounter Selma on their way home from town. There Tom's identity as buccaneer, as one who left owing money and more, is revealed along with the possibility that Tom has left a legacy in insurance money and a further hint that Lois may be his daughter. Later, Hawkins Ryden describes his cousin Tommy as one who " 'never paid for all of nothing in his life' "; and Rooster (who has already seen Milo's likeness to Tom) says " 'Amen' " (99) to that, preparing the ground for our equation of Tommy Ryden with Kate's Tom.

From beyond the grave, Tom attempts finally to pay his debts; and the force of his ghostly will explains that atmosphere of premonition and fate which surrounds Milo's day. Though Milo asserts that he can be named for Milo the Greek wrestler rather than his kin if he prefers, an uncanny resemblance to Tom overrides any intention of Milo's and transforms him into an agent for the past. Genetic and supernatural determinism are both at work here, for Milo is kin to Tommy and their resemblance is also temporarily augmented by the ghost's need. That theme of necessity versus free will is enforced by numerous references to Judgment Day and to the harsh workings of an Old Testament God. Dr. Fuller brands Warrenton a Nineveh, recalling how Jonah had attempted to escape God's plan for him and failed; Mr. Favro recites the fate of Jezebel, eaten by dogs; and Kate's favorite Bible story is of Jephthah's daughter, sacrificed because of her father's blind covenant with God. All three of these stories relate the inexorable progress of forces outside man's control.

Milo's arrival on Kate's doorstep is therefore no accident. He is led there by Rooster and indirectly by Tom, who had declared to Selma that Death " 'will be my spirit and carry my messages to you from the grave' " (102). Milo subordinates a wish to assert his own identity and becomes Tom for Kate. Sexually, he becomes Tom's snake: there are references to his phallus as " 'the messenger boy' " (184) and the "prodigal returned" (161). When Milo exhorts his penis to rise, "as if it were a coward in battle" (159), he is also overcoming Rooster's disability in order to redeem the failures of both men. Their lovemaking is described in terms of vegetation imagery— "his spade," for instance, forces Kate "into bloom" (165)—as the seed of the baby which Tom had promised and of Rooster's heir is planted. That imagery combines with the definition of Rooster as the Apple King—Pomeroy in " 'the language of love' " (95)—to suggest that Milo has not only made good on the rooster's crowing, but also restored to the Fisher King (or sheriff) his right of office. "Tom's spadework" (163) is also Rooster's.

Throughout the novel we are unsure of the degree of sympathy that should be granted to Tom. As Emma remarks, Tom " 'paid for *freedom* with his life' " (99). Apparently, he continues to be punished by God for making the wrong choice, opting for freedom instead of responsibility either to his family (Rooster's initial choice, which he regrets) or to the pitiful women whose love he compelled. But perhaps any of these choices would have led to regret. Perhaps the wisdom to seize the right woman when she presents herself is the only answer: Rooster implies as much in saying that " 'nine girls out of ten' " (129) cause the ruin of male lives. We cannot know whether Tom's wish to be detained even in a prison, to give and receive love, would ever have become more powerful than his impulse toward flight. Were Tom and Kate capable of being the exception for each other? Are Milo and Lois? Our uncertainty is parallel to Milo's in knowing how to use what he learns from Tom and from trapped men like Yancey and his own father.

Kate's uncertainty about Tom led to his disappearance—or would he have abandoned her in any case, leaving the child he had wanted as a souvenir? Kate was waiting (like Selma and Lois) for a man to rescue her from a life she hated: " 'When I wasn't crying . . . I was praying, telling the Lord I would give Him a year to repay me for His awful mistake or I would take measures' " (169). To ask is not necessarily to receive, or to get what one has bargained for—as the story of Jephthah's daughter shows. Tom came as God's gift, or His judgment on Kate's arrogant prayer. The unresolved nature of their relationship has kept Mrs. Pomeroy under Tom's spell for thirteen years. And Milo releases her from that, indicating how the sexual act can fulfill dreams and end them. Kate's readiness to welcome an impotent husband implies her acceptance of God's plan as well as of the man who gave his blood for her instead of freedom. There is also the chance that Rooster's impotence will cease now that Tom's ghost has left his bed.

The Ghost (Part Two)

The arrival of Tommy Ryden's ghost is subtly prepared for by references to a living Bible, to Judgment, and to persons long dead. We are told, for instance, that the fate of Milo the Greek wrestler was to be attacked by wolves, and wolves are now circling the fairgrounds; that the death of Milo's father (whose drunkenness he revives) was a form of Judgment; and that Milo's arrival as Tom is taken by Kate for Judgment. The biblical past is also present, in the imagination of the characters, and in that Dr. Fuller is linked to Jonah, Milo to Judas, and Kate to Jephthah's daughter. Such associations with the living dead are typically related to the theme of

Judgment because the need to assess past examples of human life is determined by that continuing threat.

More obvious preparations for the ghost include Milo's vision of Rooster, a black family's claim that the Ryden homeplace is hexed, and Rosacoke's strange pursuit of Milo. Both her imaginative journey to Lois's door and her resemblance to a girl outside Kate's house suggest a magical extension of Rosa's concern for Milo. But the line between actual and metaphorical supernaturalism intentionally wavers. Lois, for instance, seems to possess some of her father's corporeal versatility when she disappears "smoky as if she had been snatched away or had vanished in anguish like a speechless ghost" (56). In another instance Milo flings the "wolfish skull of a murdered weasel" against a tree so hard that it explodes and sends down "a flying squirrel like its sudden ghost" (132). Milo, furthermore, does considerably more floating than gravity would permit. Sometimes an otherworldly touch is humorous, as when Macey (to enforce Death's dual identity) poses as " 'a *holy* snake,' " a visitor from " 'the Great Beyond' " (114); and sometimes it is serious, as when Lois predicts with accuracy the futures of Papa, Rooster, Rosa, and Milo. Even the "worthless and beautiful" (131) things which are found during the hunt—a crazy turtle, glittering mica, oyster shells from "God-knew-where" (132), and the weasel's skull—are proof that we inhabit an extraordinary world.

After his interlude with Kate, Milo intends to rejoin the posse at the Ryden place. His journey is interrupted, however, by a flat tire. As an answer to Milo's prayer, "a dark man" appears with a lantern and the lug wrench that Milo requires. Milo's repetition of Macey's ghostly " 'Whooo' " (188) signals the unusual nature of this visitor who stammers "like someone rusty for talk" (189); in the age-old fashion of ghosts, he can recall neither his name nor his destination. Still he manages to get them both to the abandoned Ryden home, set among trees "dark as any grave" (193), on a stormy evening which seems stage-managed for a ghost's return. Tom's lantern at this point becomes critical. Milo's burgeoning sexual powers have been referred to as "a rising light that could stunt, sear"; a black girl has said to a boy " '*Lead* kindly light' " (20); and Milo now identifies himself as " 'Kindly light' " (193) when he takes Tom's lantern. Clearly, Tom's light has in the past been destructive for the women who followed it. His intention is to repair that damage, as he enabled Milo to repair that tire. But Milo announces a plan to make love to

Lois, and the reformed ghost nearly kills him with the lug wrench.
First he asks Milo, " 'That's what you call giving?' " (199), and
Milo can think of nothing else he has to give but blood—a com-
modity which both Rooster and Tom have given in abundance. Soon
Tom will lead Milo to bestow money as his gift to Lois; but now, to
protect his daughter, the ghost sheds Milo's blood and touches it as
if "blood were money."

The ghost's amnesia has by this time been largely cured. In some
murky fashion Tom contemplates the insurance money he earned with
his blood as he touches Milo's. He seeks divine pardon for killing
his " 'own blood cousin' " (200), reveals his motive, and asks " 'Am
I *sent* at last to give my gift or must I still roam?' " (201). Tom's
speech, we are told, is heard "in two places": "in the room itself"
(so the ghost is real) and "in Milo's bloody head, a sleeping vision"
(200). A swelling light replaces that of the lantern, consumes Tom,
seals Milo's wound, leads him to "the privy no larger than a grave,"
and is replaced by Death. The snake attacks and in its coil Milo yells
Tom's name "to his own surprise but not to the snake's" (202). Milo
is then saved from his wrestling match with the angel of death by
Rooster's gun—just as the sheriff's life with Kate was saved by Milo's
phallic " 'loaded gun' " (87).

The light that travels between Milo, Tom, and Death suggests the
ghost's ability to become manifest in any required form. And the
spirit's presence is in no way lessened by the demise of the snake, for
there is still confusion over the rightful beneficiary to Tom's money,
which has descended from the ceiling with Death. The atmosphere
of miracles continues, as Papa bends "from the waist with no sign
of pain—something he had not done in Milo's lifetime" (204), and
as Milo lifts fifty pounds of dead snake "like a fistful of feathers"
(208) to get to Rooster's ear. The tableau recalls a Judas "kiss," for
Milo threatens to betray Rooster if he fails to dispose properly of the
money. It sometimes happens, as with Rosa and Milo (whom she had
called Judas), that it is necessary to betray one trust in order to keep
another. That harsh truth echoes through the novel, confirming the
difficulty of Milo's day. Now the light is in Rooster's hands—for only
the law can ensure that Lois receives Tom's legacy.

Throughout the novel light has functioned as energy—sexual, supernatural, and dramatic. It moves according to who is in the spotlight,
according to where the energy centers at any given moment. It comes
from God, as Macey implies when the light strikes through "an un-

leaved hole in the trees" (110), so that often the light—like Death, or the money—seems to descend through a ceiling that separates God and man. Thus it is God's gift or His Judgment, proof of a link between the two worlds. Now the light passes from Rooster to Lois, who leads Milo to the car and uses it to see "the face that shone beneath his own with a light not his." In a trance, she says to her father " 'I have met you . . . where I promised I would' " (214). The promise fulfilled, the light dies in Milo's face, and the two continue "in total dark—light dead in her hand"(215).

Back at the Mustian home, Selma begins at Milo's insistence a partial account of the events leading up to Kate's encounter with Tom. "A presence unseen as air but offended, potentially hurtful" presses upon Milo in response to Selma's denial of her true role. Seeing "Milo's face being finally, fully Tom's from within," Selma corrects her story—leaving Milo "free, dispossessed, also abandoned" (230). On cue, Rooster arrives to dispose of the money issue; Milo, no longer the vessel for Tom's spirit, is unable to recall anything of use. Selma's timely intervention elicits yet another (Rooster's) version of the Ryden tale, and Lois is awarded both the money and the truth that Selma is her mother.

The Resolution (Part Three)

The last thirty pages of the novel are a refutation of the romantic dimensions of the tale. Milo has risen to heights that he cannot sustain, as the novel's epigraph from Dante's *Purgatorio* makes clear: " 'How hast thou deigned to climb the hill? / Didst thou not know that man is happy here?' "[4] This epigraph, however, also implies that the elevation allowed to Dante and to Milo in the romance is a foretaste of the divinely comic ending which may follow death. Again this section opens with Milo rising from sleep. He had ended the previous day by collapsing in exhaustion on Baby Sister's bed, having meant to answer her question about love—"to tell, warn, delight her" (244). But his role as messenger is at an end. The death of Milo's day suggested by that collapse is underscored by the fact that Milo has returned to his habitually dreamless state, and perhaps still more by the dream he does have "of rest—a walk through shade or stretched in green woods, shielded from day." This image may recall Charlemagne's knight Roland, who expires in a wood; like that fallen knight, Milo has been laid to rest by his friends, by Rooster who

"had carried him up in his arms." No light—either in the dream or
in the darkness to which Milo awakes—is now finding its way through
God's ceiling. We may also be reminded of that shattered figure in
Keats's "La Belle Dame Sans Merci" who awakes like Milo, torn
between thinking himself healed and *"deathly* sick" (245) now that
the dream is past.

Lois stands at Milo's door, offering sexual thanks for her knight's
travail. And he rejects her: " 'I was nearly killed for *taking* once
already. I am meant to give.' " Milo has yet to learn that "givers and
takers need not be separate" (246). The articulation of this thought
is strategically placed, for Lois now departs and Milo has a vision of
various others leaving, of the numerous unresolved relationships which
he has witnessed. In all of these cases pain is incurred through an
act of giving that cannot for one reason or another be reciprocated.
Milo understands both that he must allow Lois to give her thanks
and that he does not want to lose her; his fear of Tommy's wrath
ends, too, because Milo has a better grasp of what giving means.
"The chance—the certainty—of loss" (248), coupled with the sound
of footsteps, "Lois surely, dressed and leaving" (247), moves Milo to
seek Lois in haste.

In the kitchen, however, he is stopped by news of Rato's apparent
death. That ultimate departure suggests that Milo will be unable to
expiate the guilt of several failures to help Rato. Responding to Mr.
Favo's eulogy of Rato, Milo echoes a speech he made to Kate concerning the choice he would make between solitude and connection.
Whereas to Kate he has implied that both choices are viable, Milo
now rejects through his description of Rato's habitual isolation a life
in which one could " 'never look forward to . . . giving somebody
something' " (253). He seems to have learned, as Kate thought
should be easy with Tom's example, " 'to recognize the Lord when
He comes, . . . [to] know what message you are bearing' " (184).
God's message may be translated as an insistence upon generous love,
a denial of His blessing upon the buccaneer's life. But the point is
complicated by Selma's reference to " 'what Jesus intended' "—that
men could leave their families in pursuit of an ideal and " 'never look
back.' " Rooster's response to that was " 'Jesus ought to been shot' "
(236), presumably for confusing the issue. Now in the kitchen,
Rooster and Milo stand as opponents of isolation or departure; but
to choose as they have done is still not proof against loss. That point
is made resoundingly when, as Rooster claims that the sun must rise

again today because he needs to get home to Kate, Mr. Favro answers
" 'that's no reason at all' " (256). God's will is absolute, and the
existence of debts does not establish an opportunity to repay. Death
or Judgment can come at any time, and our errors may be permanent.
We are not to expect that the miraculous dispensations of Milo's day
are available on demand.

For Milo, the opportunity that Lois seems to offer is still at hand.
Mr. Favro warns that " 'there are others here that need you more' "
(255), but Milo chooses Lois. They make love, "pure gift for both,
no thought of receipt though receipts poured in" (265–66); and
strangely, they conclude this act with a mutual sense of having been
"spared" from what had seemed "a new clear life" together "so long
as [they] moved" (266). As at Kate's house, an adolescent dream is
fulfilled and ended. Perhaps Milo and Lois were not the exception for
each other and only hoped otherwise because of the need for connection which was illustrated so powerfully around them. In any case,
the author provides an experience of mutual gift and an aftertaste of
freedom so that their relationship can be resolved. Price is limited,
of course, by Milo's unfortunate marriage to Sissie in *A Long and
Happy Life*. If the suggestion is that Milo and Lois are saved from
an unhappy life together, there is no assurance that happiness will
reside elsewhere.

Milo has two remaining choices, to stay with his family or go off
alone. The former choice is modified by a recognition that eventually
he would marry and pursue " 'what nine-tenths of the humans born
since God said 'Adam!' have thought was a life' " (269)—Sissie, of
course, is one of Rooster's " 'nine girls out of ten.' " Milo inclines
toward departure, but lets it depend on whether Rato is really dead.
His reason for leaving is not to escape Yancey's or his father's fate,
but to " 'wrestle' " (272) his way toward a life and to tell what he
knows. Price does not clarify the means of telling, but we may assume that he is thinking of the artist's choice. Perhaps only that would
accommodate the full burden of Milo's day, its conflicting evidence;
only the artist goes and in imagination stays; only he can "warn [and]
delight" (244) us with pictures of human love. Milo, however, is not
an artist. He is incapable of changing lives. The light now shines
only on Milo's back, his day is over, and he cannot articulate to Lois
what he knows.

At this juncture, Phillip and Rato come home. Milo's fate is sealed,
a fate he was willing to accept if God indicated by this return that

there might be some few compensations. A pattern of wolf-related imagery which culminates here suggests, however, that such mercies as this are not to be relied upon. Rato has lost his shirt " 'in a fight with a fox' " (274), and Milo cannot "shield" Rato forever from the "black rake of claws" whose threat is merely "postponed" (275). Everywhere is the death's head, the *memento mori* of that mad dog's head that Dr. Fuller carried or the wolfish skull that Milo had contemplated as if it were Yorick's. The dogs that devour Jezebel or the wolves that destroy Milo the wrestler are synonymous with "the hound that had sought [Milo] since his father's death but closely, fiercely all weekend—that people depart (undetained by love, unprepared for their journey) and we watch them go and they do not return" (266). Like Rato, Milo has escaped death this time: the hounds which descended on the privy were not for him. But Milo is wrong to have consoled himself with the news that his Greek wrestler was destroyed only after a long life. Milo is still fifteen, and there are six hours left of morning, but death—either literal or figurative—can attack at any time, as God wills.

Chapter Five
Love and Work
Introduction and Plot Summary

In *Love and Work* Price leaves the Mustian family behind. He abandons the charm and comic surface they had provided in order to plunge more deeply, nakedly, and painfully into that dialectic between solitude and connection from which all his work springs. Many reviewers mourned or were irritated by the change. Essentially, their charge was that Price had exchanged the lamp of fiction for the mirror (only slightly distorted) of autobiography. This novel does rely more closely than the Mustian books on the author's own experience; it uses, for instance, the reported appearance of his father's ghost to his mother, just before her aneurysm burst. But the autobiographical impulse works variously in the making of fiction, so that *Love and Work* is not the strange, unheralded departure some readers have supposed. Moreover, it is fiction—a transformation of fact, as all powerful creative work must be.

The opposition between love and work as these are experienced by Thomas Eborn is particularly an artist's version of the debate between connection and freedom which was apparent in the Mustian novels. Like Price, Eborn is a writer and a teacher; like Price again, he is more sophisticated than his parents or the people around whom he lived as a child. Although both reside (slightly distanced) in the region of their childhoods, that environment has altered in two distinct ways. First, it has been invaded by the ugly forces of urbanism— "literal cancers (proliferation of unneeded cells)"[1]—to which both author and character are firmly opposed; and this threat to place is understood as parallel to the ravages of time and disease which destroy Eborn's parents. Despite the sensibility that Eborn displays in his own writing and in his taste for Wordsworth, there is an urban sickness (a lack of rootedness) at work in his spirit. Secondly, as their university affiliations suggest, both Price and Eborn inhabit another, more cosmopolitan world which is superimposed upon their rural pasts.

In *Love and Work*, then, Price is writing out of a fairly recent period of his life. The Mustian novels are set earlier—Milo's day occurs in 1948, when Price also was fifteen; and he draws there upon the sort of young people "who were imported into the Warrenton school by bus each day from surrounding farms." In the portraits of Rosacoke and Milo he records his dismay at how "an extraordinary fineness" of youth would be blasted by "what lay over-whelmingly in wait"[2] for many of the rural adolescents he had known. The Mustian children did not have the option of some valuable external work on which to base their freedom. Thomas Eborn does; and Price, in *Love and Work*, examines the case of a person rather more like himself to assess the costs of that more privileged existence.

Related to the charge of self-absorption made by several of the book's reviewers was an attack on Price's style. One critic deplored the novel's "self-consciousness" and "relentless overwriting";[3] another thought "its language grotesquely swollen and vainglorious"[4] and added that the extravagance of metaphor was often meaningless. But when Price refers to Eborn as "furred with dread" (5) he is attempting a visceral and precise description, not obfuscation. Moreover, the slow care of Price's style, its straining after accuracy, is particularly geared to his subject: Eborn's idiom is Price's and both are engaged in a serious, complex exploration. For readers who follow it closely *Love and Work* must appear as a remarkably compact and precise achievement.

In Part One of the novel Eborn is writing an essay about the value of work when his mother telephones, and he refuses the call. To make amends, he goes to his mother's house and finds it empty; he is joined by Ida, who says that her friend's aneurysm has burst. Soon after Eborn's arrival at the hospital, his mother dies, and he returns home to complete the essay. In Part Two Eborn's wife Jane reads his essay and is insulted by its implicit dismissal of their life together. Eborn burns his mother's papers in order to sever his ties with her and then is witness to a fatal automobile accident—which realizes a dream he has had, caused by his wish to clear space for his own work. At dinner with friends, he is finally horrified by his coldness. In Part Three he begins a novel about his parents which he hopes will reconcile love and work. Jane calls the scene he reads to her " 'Easy lies' " (108). Their marriage now in serious jeopardy, the Eborns learn that someone has broken into his mother's house. In Part Four, with two policemen, they find that a coil of human excrement has been deposited in the kitchen. Then Ida arrives to reveal the purpose of his mother's call, to inform Eborn that his father's ghost had appeared. And she claims that now both ghosts have returned. Eborn sees them. He realizes that their love excludes him, that his parents have no need of his work as a memorial to lives that were sufficient in a way his can never be.

Eborn's Character

The man who refuses his mother's phone call is not always an attractive character, even to himself. Thus the reference to Eborn as a "migrained duchess" (3) comes essentially from his own satirical voice. The gender he employs is instructive, for Eborn thinks men should have greater equilibrium. That point is made again when he condemns Dorothy Wordsworth for her madness, saying that "Your mind is your own" (18). Later, he thinks of himself as Cordelia, unwilling to express her love for Lear although it cost her a kingdom. In the accident scene Eborn seems to blame himself for a female squeamishness, a lack of manly courage. And his sexual responses to Jane are also problematic: he must feign orgasm, and he is apparently disgusted by their lovemaking. What all this amounts to is considerable self-doubt. On the one hand, Eborn sees love as chaotic and a woman's business, and the work to which he has retreated as a manly discipline. He is afraid of the female in himself, which would expose him to the risks of betrayal and impermanence. On the other hand, he is aware that this retreat may have been motivated by fear, and so he questions the manliness of his choice.

Eborn's self-loathing alternates with self-admiration. After his guilt about his mother is roused, Eborn lashes out at his essay: "Turbid concealment—as was all his work. Concealment of what? A hole in the heart" (14). But when he decides to visit his mother, Eborn immediately feels much better, good enough to indulge in light-hearted narcissism before the shaving mirror and to criticize others. Ironically, he blames students for not understanding what Wordsworth means by love; and he describes egalitarian America as "barnacled already, past scraping, with deceit; sinking slowly from the sheer weight of hot air but savagely swelling, a wallowing balloon" (17). As one critic has observed, that image might apply to Eborn, scraping off his beard, indulging in hot air and deceit, as his mother's aneurysm is ballooning.[5] The point is that his satisfaction escalates into feelings of superiority with alarming speed. A quick fear of

Jane's death illustrates the rhythm of Eborn's life, for in the next instant he is considering an essay on narcissism as a function of beardlessness. Anything that passes through Eborn's mind, it seems, is worthy of writing up—and his own situation is the perennial subject. No longer sure the work essay has failed, Eborn is nevertheless "aware that his mood of quick elation stood on silly sand" (19). Throughout the novel we observe Eborn's vacillation between despair and overweening pride in the work he values above all.

A thoroughly literary man, Eborn is given to frequent literary allusions and to criticism of the written word. He is linked to Narcissus, Odysseus, Tristan (abandoned by Isolde, who figures as Eborn's mother), Christ and Cordelia. All of the literary talk in the novel applies somehow to Eborn's situation, and his responses to a variety of events and documents involving his mother signal an excessively literary approach to life. When she is taken to Intensive Care, he thinks that would make a good title for a Russian novel; as the doctor approaches to announce death, Eborn is curious about what style he will adopt. He reacts against the sentimentality of several entries in the diary his mother kept during the period of his father's death, although he approves of some of her literary techniques. What he dislikes is the falsity of such sentiment: his father's claim " 'that you are mine and I am yours' " (27) in a letter to Eborn's mother, or the verse pinned to his mother's jewelry box, asserting that *"when you help a fellow up a steep hill, / you get nearer to the top yourself"* (119). But both of these are sentiments from which Eborn is peculiarly cut off; and what would sound trite in literature can be sincerely felt (and even true) in life.

Imagery

Eborn dislikes being touched, physically or by sentiment. When Ida says that his mother's message must have been of love, Eborn blames his "reeling, in revulsion" on "Ida's sopped smile" (30). He must force himself to touch Ida or Jane. In the hospital he fears infection from a boy in the elevator, and when the doctor squeezes his knee in sympathy, "helpless it shied" (38). Such references develop into a pattern of withdrawal, spatially conceived, and referring particularly to houses. Driving to his mother's house after the first phone call, Eborn finds that "forces stronger than his own guilty will had taken control and were reeling him in . . . *won* not *caught*"

(19). But when he gets there, Eborn's impulse (and later his action) is to strip that house, the "top-heavy barge groaning with debris" (20), which is the image of his mother's life. He realizes from one dream that he is wishing destruction on others so that he will have "room to turn" (31), and in another dream he reacts with rage to hordes of people invading his house. He wants head space, "sufficient room" (60) to think of his work. But also occupying his head are "the hungry dead" (74) whom he first resists and then attempts to propitiate with his work.

When he goes to clean out his mother's house, Eborn rejoices to see that ivy has broken through the wall: it means that " 'this has all surrendered' " and that his throat is "free from all the hands that held it" (55). Jane also has tears which are "instruments of entry—crowbars" (49) invading him, and when later he feels the need of his mother's house Jane is seen as "the breaker, the ravenous thief" (115) who not only destroys their own lives and his work, but also erases his mother's imprint from the sheets because of jealousy. The distance that Eborn has desired becomes frightening to him. Feeling his coldness, a reaction to the pressure of others, Eborn flees from the dinner table on the night of the accident, and imagines himself as "locked in frigid mineral of meteor . . . trapped and hurtling with only two hopes: impact and explosion or perpetual fall" (73). Continuing that metaphor, he thinks of "our only tether, the past" from which he has cut himself "adrift" (74). The novel about his parents is Eborn's effort to establish some proximity to love, and even when Jane has revealed the spurious element in his work Eborn thinks: "A houseless man, if he's seen roof and walls, can still build a house. Had better." The void threatens, and as Eborn walks toward the second phone call announcing housebreakers he feels "whirled at the sick circumference of loss" (109). "At the rim of his mind," Eborn resents Jane's offer to go with him; "but at core he was clung to all that now mattered—the house had been breeched, maybe final damage done" (112). The meteor image is again recalled when Eborn cannot bear "his arid stopped life (dry-farming, the culture of plants on the airless moon)" or find the energy required for "severing Jane or abiding her in pithed proximity" (117).

Related to such images is the door, which appears in the first sentence of the novel: "The phone's first ring pierced his study door, a klaxon vs. cheap birch veneer" (3). The call is seen as an invasion of Eborn's space, the door as insufficient barrier to his mother and

wife. That closed door is reminiscent of Rosacoke's and Milo's wish
for privacy in the Mustian novels, recalled again when we discover
that as an adolescent Thomas Eborn had placed a Yale lock on his
bedroom door. At the end of Part One Eborn feels a ghostly pressure mounting in his study, and to release it he opens the door.
When Jane tells Tom to look at (meaning to consider) his mother,
he actually looks at an open, empty "dimly-lit door" (51). And
when the ghost of Todd Eborn appears to his wife Lou, he is described
as " 'looking towards the door' " (141). Thus it seems that the door
is a passageway to another world, and that access to the supernatural
may begin with a willingness to keep the door open to love. In the
accident scene a mysterious pregnant woman appears in her open
doorway, to help by phoning for the police and ambulance, and
later by insisting on Eborn's innocence; but she will not venture out
because she believes that to come too close would mark her unborn
child. Governed by superstition, that vague figure in the door connects with the ghost of Eborn's mother and with Jane, who is also
" 'loyal to [her] superstitions' " (133) and barren as a sign of Eborn's
sterility. While there is no legal question of Eborn's guilt, his spiritual
complicity in such destruction would end if he could accept the
life-bearing message of the woman in the door.

A still more subtle use of the door image appears in Eborn's essay
on work, where he tries to remove that taint of words that *"Hitler
inscribed across the one-way gates into his death camps*: Arbeit Macht
Frei—*Work Makes Free*" (9). Because Hitler so often succeeded in
parting those loving couples who walked through his door (a point
which Price elaborates in "Waiting at Dachau"), this door is opposed
to the one through which Todd and Lou Eborn vanish (and return)
together. But if Thomas had converted them to his faith in work over
love, they might have gone instead (as he does) through Hitler's
"one-way gates."

The Work Essay

The night before Eborn writes his essay, he dreams that Ted (his
young colleague) and three of his students are in an automobile
accident. Bloody, they enter a hotel lobby where he stands, and then
pass through "solid doors" beyond his reach. In the hospital he cannot recall their names, but "the success of his artistry" (4) in
description leads to a phone conversation with Cal (his best student)

revealing that "all were divided, all gravely hurt but him" (5). To disprove the dream, he first telephones to Cal and then writes the essay he had promised for Cal's magazine. The pomposity of which Eborn is painfully, defiantly aware is evident in the ironic manner of his speech to Cal, whose phone is answered by a girl: " 'Sorry to wake you and your lovely guest but we oldsters rise early.' " Thus he calls the essay "square but true," and begins it as a "thank-offering for the dream disproved, charm against its return or delayed explosion" (6). He denies through the celebration of work, however, not so much the destruction of his friends as the dream's image of himself as powerless and guilty. His second justification for the essay is a photograph of his parents, revealing to Eborn their vulnerability—and that motive also quickly becomes less generous. A tender, hopeless wish to protect those once-youthful figures from death becomes a harsh assessment of their lives, a belief that their "boredom, futility . . . puzzlement" (8) was caused by the absence of any valuable work. His essay will show their mistake.

In this essay Eborn argues that work frees us from a dependence on others, which is crippling because they always fail us by betrayal or death. Work provides something else to care about, if skillfully done. It is a justification for self-love as well as a means of passing the time without being overcome by panic or self-hatred. It is a shield from dangers without and within. Work may not change our weaknesses, but at least it will exercise our strengths. In work we create order. Outside of work is the chaos of our failure to live well. This paraphrase makes rather more of the writer's personal "flaws" as his motive for seeking the protection of work than the essay strictly requires. But it suggests the interpretation toward which Eborn moves when he is blaming himself for having refused his mother's phone call and which the novel as a whole confirms. Eborn judges his essay first as "square wind"; secondly as "the privatest, most local of truths; meaningless to anyone less desperate than he or desperate in other ways"; and thirdly as "turbid concealment" of his "hole in the heart" (14).

Although Eborn does not retract the "hole" in his heart, he later adds that one of the things work has freed him for, *"though for moments only,"* is the chance *"to round on myself, stand, face my own failure; and survive the sight"* (41). That statement is particularly interesting since his essay was published separately by Price under his own name. We may think the essay expresses Price's own views without Eborn's emphasis on the hole in his heart. Or we may assume that Price, in creating Eborn, chooses not to conceal—indeed, surely to exaggerate—his own most "loyal" flaw, a distrust of love. Perhaps this is the secret of all Price's work. He begins with a belief that art should change lives, then urges himself toward that one vital change (trust in love) in everything he writes. Or, perhaps, feeling that he cannot change his life, he offers this work instead. In either case, is he making a cowardly retreat from life or facing it as bravely as he can? That surely is Eborn's question, and we cannot avoid thinking it is also a question for Price.

Lou's Death and the Accident

Eborn's attitude to his mother (Lou) is captured in the extreme image of a "two-edged" axe of "incest and matricide' (58). Prior to his mother's death, Eborn reflects on this paradox: "She was his, at last, all but totally. And he no longer needed or wanted her." Recalling how Lou had indulged his "child's lust" (14), Eborn deplores his fickleness; but he dwells on her loss of physical attractiveness as if it were a betrayal of his former love. That his mother has exchanged her matrimonial bed for Eborn's, "scene of his raging puberty" (23), makes him feel both "eviction and encounter, longing and repugnance" (22). He cannot decide whether to blame her or himself for the cessation of his desire and is furthermore unsure whether that desire has really ended. At her deathbed Eborn wrests the wedding ring from Lou's finger—having been asked by the nurses if he knows the combination, the way out of wedlock. Thus he collaborates in her dishonoring, with the impersonal nurses who treat her now like debris, although his original impulse had been to save her from such indignity. Satisfied that the ring is now his, Eborn believes that he has succeeded in separating his parents; he kisses the ring, but he also wills his mother's death. Later that afternoon, however, Eborn has a second dream of loss. A van crowded with children invades his home; he recognizes that "their guides are his parents," but "they do not see him or hear him when he sobs, abandoned, violated" (43). This dream painfully reveals his parents as still united (as in the photograph, they even dress alike) and Eborn as the rejected instead of the rejecting child. Further, they seem to prefer other children, who will accept their guidance as he does not.

The accident scene is preceded by Eborn's burning of his mother's papers. The house is now as "safe . . . as a field swept of mines," and he is "a lighter man, stripped by force of will, scraped clean as a keel, aimed for his work" (59). The accident threatens Eborn's satisfaction in that impulse that caused him to burn the papers and that now seems to have wreaked further destruction as a fulfillment of his dream. Throughout this harrowing (and brilliantly written) scene Eborn is reluctant—out of "fear? indifference?" (65)—to offer help. A more humane response comes from two mysteriously ordinary figures, the woman in the door and the policeman. With great subtlety, Price implies a supernatural grace in the policeman's arrival and treatment of the dying boy, whom he tells to say an " *'Our Father'* " (67). Ashamed at having done so little to help, Eborn accepts responsibility for that by telling the boy his name and asking his pardon. But he is not altogether sorry. He leaves thinking that such destruction will end " 'When I let it. . . . When I've stripped all attachments from myself; stand clean of my family, hindering strangers; stand alone, my own' " (69). Only at dinner that night is Eborn finally appalled by the conditions which his work had seemed to require.

The Novel

Eborn's decision to begin a novel about his parents comes when he has acknowledged both the need to "anchor his own flapping life" (79) and that the dead "easily steer" (75) our present lives. He wishes to build again the ravaged house, the scuttled ship. Ted's poem in honor of Lou gives him the idea; he wants to do a better job, to arrive at "the total discoveries available only to donkey-prose, the longer journey, the diurnal haul." In particular, he thinks that the failure of Ted's "lovely" poem is to reveal "the Bethlehem Mary, not the baffled widow of Nazareth, abandoned" (79). When Jane calls his effort " 'Easy lies,' " Eborn's first, instinctive defense is that he has not finished ("the diurnal haul" has just begun), and his second is that his parents' " 'ugliest chances' " (108) have been glimpsed even in these early pages. With his preference for the "baffled widow," the latter defense suggests that Eborn's vision is still intensely dark, and that he has not yet seen the *"light"* (143) which is generated by his parents' love. That may be the distortion of his work to which Jane reacts, its obsessive concern with loss, which is perhaps, as Eborn had feared, "the privatest, most local of truths." But Jane's enigmatic phrase is more readily explained in her own terms. She says " 'your scene and everything you've said' " are " 'Easy lies' " (108) because she is offended by Eborn's claim that his work is a tribute to love. It is easier for Eborn to write about love than to practice it, but still impossible, Jane thinks, for him to portray love accurately when he does not understand it.

Neither the obsessive darkness of Eborn's vision nor his personal failures in love in fact vitiate the scenes that he reads to Jane. Her judgment may be defensible in either regard, but it is certainly harsh. Eborn's parents are shown at the beginning of their courtship, with Lou attracted by Todd's physical grace as Rosa was by Wesley's in *A Long and Happy Life*. On skates, Todd withdraws for once from obligations to his needy family and from a girl who clings to him without the pride Lou exhibits. The danger of his wish to be a buccaneer is shown by the fear that he will skate over the falls, or that the car will crash, and by his attraction to bootleg liquor. When Todd pretends to be shot, Lou (whose parents are dead) thinks " *Lost . . . They all fly from me* " (101). But she also sees *"her own need and readiness for ruin"* and understands that *"death is not the only fear"* (100). Other familiar motifs are Todd's ability to change into another person (like the father's in "The Names and Faces of Heroes"), Lou's waiting, and the elaborate play on who leads and who follows in a walk through woods. That Price should offer as Eborn's work an unmistakable sample of his own preoccupations, and then attack it through Jane, is further evidence of his willingness in *Love and Work* to confront a negative image of the self.

Jane

Jane's role in the novel is problematic mainly because her characterization is rather thin. We cannot tell how far she is a latter-day Lou and how far she participates with Eborn in a contemporary malaise. Remarking on the "near impossibility" of married love in the American middle classes, Price describes Eborn and Jane as "this very self-important, whey-faced pair of intellectuals who are . . . struggling through their attempt to have a little modern marriage, 'a meaningful relationship.' "[6] He seems, therefore, to believe that attempt is doomed. The only hope Price offers—"their single chance, single guarantee, of continuation" (129), if not of happiness—is the

fact that Jane cries (her tears like grace) when she sees the excrement. But if Price obviously honors the marriage he assigns to
Eborn's parents and satirizes the "little modern marriage" of Eborn
and Jane, that opposition is confused by Jane's emphatically tradi-
tional view of woman's work. She tells Eborn that " 'we are my work' "
and that the life of every woman " 'barring the bitches' " is to serve
man as "janitor, cook, nurse, mother, laundress, yawning thighs' "
(51). And despite Jane's sophistication, there are numerous indica-
tions of her willingness to serve Eborn in these capacities, so that the
probable failure of the marriage would seem to rest almost entirely
with him.

The problem may be mainly sexual. Jane is willing to be the love-
centered woman that Lou was, but Eborn cannot tolerate another
woman in his mother's place. Jane's jealousy of Lou is in these circumstances perfectly explicable. In the scene where Eborn feigns
orgasm, he must conceal "his loathing, the picture that hung in his
eyes of them both hitched glaborous together" (52), a picture which
is then replaced by a considerably more attractive "vision of his father
and mother, locked to a bed, their joined hips hacking out signals of
love as they worked to unite their lovely skins" (53). There is some
suggestion that Jane also has given "a skilled fake," but that may be
projection on Eborn's part. This is the only dramatized scene of their
lovemaking, although Eborn recalls "the self-conscious Rabelaisian
affirmation that late afternoon [of his mother's death], frantic ball-
and-socket drill in the face of death" (52). That reference, however,
seems a mistake since on that occasion Eborn had rejected Jane's
overture. Eborn's sexual distaste for Jane is revealed again when the
hatred unleashed by her rejection of his work takes the form first of
his despising the "love-equipment" (113) she may have packed, and
then of indulging in an ugly pun on the word " 'coming' " (115). We
are not told whose decision or incapacity is responsible for their childlessness. But the ghost scene suggests that in any case this is a symbol
rather than a cause of their marital failure, for there we are reminded
by Ida of what Lou Eborn also knew—that " 'people come in pairs not
threes or fives' " (137).

The Ghosts

The supernaturalism that was so prominent in *A Generous Man* is
in *Love and Work* even more daring, since the tone of this novel is
so plainly realistic. When the ghosts appear in Part Three, we are

properly astonished. But Price has anticipated their appearance: on each occasion when Eborn was summoned to his mother's house, his car was already out; his dreams are taken as premonitory; on the afternoon of his mother's death a ghostly pressure filled Eborn's study; and he wanted to make the dead speak. Still, Eborn is essentially a realist—unlike Ida, Jane, the highway patrolman, or the woman in the doorway. When Eborn is shown the coil of excrement by two more concerned policemen, he is satisfied that this explains the housebreaking they have all come to investigate. That spectacle of human waste, however, is not the full story; the truer explanation, proof that our lives do not have to be understood so meagerly, comes when Ida reveals that his parents have returned. Although Eborn had thought "his parents' lives [were] fouled and stopped by him" (74), their return magnificently overshadows any miserly invasion by Eborn or whatever " 'bad boy' " (139) has coincidentally attempted to foul their home.

Prior to seeing the ghosts, Eborn accepts Jane's verdict that his work is both "*lies* and *easy*," on the grounds that "each word" was "fed exclusively by the one thing his parents had thought they'd learned . . . that love is possible, however scarce." He now holds that knowledge, which "he'd peddled prettily . . . in all his work, his friendships, his marriage," to be false and his parents' lie to be less culpable than his own only because it was "never unmasked" (117). Thus Eborn seems to have lost everything, the last shreds of his faith in either love or work. When he sees the ghosts, he takes them to be "the hungry dead," anxious for communication with and through him, and he is enormously relieved to think "his work, his *knowledge*, was true not lies. That at least could continue." But as the room fills with light, he realizes that they have not come for him: "He sees that, always, from the first, they have faced one another only, static in ecstasy, sealed in their needlessness, one another's goal." As he had always feared, Eborn is excluded from his parents' love—because " 'people come in pairs' " and because of his own inability to love. Their appearance means that love is possible, although not for Eborn. If he grants also that " 'The dead have their own lives' " and no need for him, then Eborn's work, which has stemmed always from the wish to justify himself before his parents, will also be finished. But these words of dismissal, "the worst he knows," are not spoken aloud, and the final implication of the novel is that Eborn will conceal them and continue to write of love: "No one has breathed" (143).

Chapter Six
Permanent Errors
Introduction

Permanent Errors is, according to Price, an "attempt to isolate in a number of lives the central error of act, will, understanding which, once made, has been permanent, incurable, but whose diagnosis and palliation are the hopes of continuance."[1] Loosely defined, it is a collection of stories divided into four parts. The first part, however, is really four stories which combine to form a discontinuous novella; the second is described by Price as "narrative poems of personal loss, therefore elegies"; the third contains one conventional story and six interrelated, surrealistic fragments; and the fourth is a novella. The "central error" throughout is a failure in love, whose "diagnosis and palliation" occur largely through art. Two of the protagonists are writers, "quasi-interchangeable lenses" (viii) with obvious optical similarities to Eborn and Price. In *Love and Work* Eborn recognizes both that " 'mistakes can be permanent' "[2] and that his work will continue. *Permanent Errors*, with its multiple perspectives and techniques all converging upon a single pattern of error, is concerned with the continuing, obsessive pattern of that error and with the compensations of art.

The epigraph for *Permanent Errors* is Price's own free translation of Rilke's "The Alchemist." An artist's parable, it draws upon a variety of alchemical traditions to describe the costs and conditions of artistic creation. Most centrally, it equates the *"crumb of gold"* that an alchemist employs as seed for his desired transmutation with the artist's own experience: he trades his life, that is, for the hope of something larger. The experiment recorded here leaves the Faustian artist *"babbling"* in disappointment, craving the life that he has sold away. But that conclusion is modified by an alchemical tradition which allows for intermediate success, and the suggestion that something of this current effort (though it falls short of the desired end) has nevertheless risen *"past him to God."* The reference to a *"crystal crib"* evokes yet another tradition, according to which the philosopher's stone is seen as a kind of homunculus, an infant born solely of the hermaphroditic alchemist; thus some defense is offered of the artist's solitude, although on this occasion his child (the work of art) is seen as a *"monster,"* born unnaturally. The artist's purpose is to become attuned perfectly with reality, to balance male and female principles, and to accept the paradox that his *"free and sovereign"* mind is *"fiercely ruled."* Finally, the epigraph serves to defend the author's choice of art as well as to admit its awful cost.

"The Happiness of Others"

"Fool's Education" is the collective title of the four stories that comprise Part One. In the first story, "The Happiness of Others," we are introduced to Charles Tamplin on the eve of his separation from Sara. An irony attaches to the definition of Tamplin as a fool, since he is an Oxford scholar securely aimed at a brilliant writing career. Put simply, Tamplin is a fool because he is willing to let Sara go, and his education involves the recognition of that error. But Tamplin's error is not an accidental one, a simple mistake of judgment; it proceeds from the kind of person he is, one who manipulates and welcomes Sara's departure so that he can get on with his work. A genuine education, therefore, would necessarily involve more than a reversal of his decision to let Sara go. He would have to relinquish enough of his self-protective pride to make space for a recalcitrant, living woman—or Sara would herself be foolish to return.

An important clue to this abiding difficulty is the motif of competition which begins in "The Happiness of Others" and becomes still more conspicuous in "Waiting for Dachau." The first story describes the efforts made by Tamplin to "kill a day as painlessly as possible" (8), his last day with Sara, which is "like a baby dumped on their doorstep, gorgeous but unwanted, condemning as an angel" (3). He rejects the sun's alchemical gilding of Sara as deceitful; he will not allow the transmutation of Sara into the object of his desire, nor will he nurture the infant day. Tamplin wants to kill time, and at first the narrative voice implies that Sara is his accomplice. Gradually, however, we discover that it is only Tamplin who rejects their union; Sara has agreed to end it precisely because that is Tamplin's deepest wish and because she desires growth and reciprocity. This difference becomes clear when Tamplin and Sara read their chosen mottoes in a church near Oxford. Tamplin recites to himself Ben Jonson's lines on the bust of Cary, which Sara has not shown the wisdom to appreciate. Jonson's poem offers the aesthetic view of life; it prefers the shapely *"small proportions"* (6) of beauty to long continuance. Sara's choice is of an aesthetically inferior poem, an epitaph for a communal grave which she discovers for the first time that day. It serves as her triumphant reply, proof that Sara has a vision of her own which spans the whole life cycle, which is available to all, and which shows love as so enduring that it can remove death's sting.

Tamplin runs from the church, reminded by Sara's lines that death *"reconciles all difference"* (7), that he will die alone and his brilliance fade to ashes. Previously, Jonson's lines had seemed "a kindness to himself," evidence that he might survive the truncation of his affair with Sara and turn it into art. He had supposed, however, that the failure of their relationship was mutual: their story, which he would tell for the rest of his life, was "only the oldest story of all— the simple entire failure to meet, to serve one another and delight in the work" (6). Now Sara has proposed another story as older and more universal: the story of love, which she charges him with having willfully destroyed. Sara dislikes Cary's bust, its features "vapid as a baby's," and charges that " 'Any man of thirty with a face bare as this, deserves to die.' " Implicitly, Tamplin is Cary—" 'half a man' " (5) because he has chosen to avoid the buffetings of life. Tamplin, retreating into art, is condemned to a living death (the denial of growth) and then to a solitary death for his refusal to endure the give-and-take of life with another person. Tamplin has refused to grant Sara's otherness, which would deflect him from a solitary course; he has been willing to accept Sara as his life's companion only on condition that she accommodate his vision entirely. And that is impossible for two reasons: Sara is an autonomous human being, with an impressive intelligence of her own, and the vision that Tamplin asks her to share is essentially a vision of love's failure.

The next scene confirms Sara's alliance with "a world older, simpler, deeper than he'd known" (11). They are out driving together, and Tamplin has retreated from "their airless symbiosis" (8) into satisfaction with the story he will make of their day when Sara again jolts him into reality. At first Tamplin does not recognize the world as hers: the sheep and "green and gold" landscape she points out are aesthetically pleasing, like " 'effects' in a nineteenth-century play." Green nature and golden art seem reconciled, a blessing designed for Tamplin. But he is vaguely perplexed by the "profitless choice" of sheep crossing the road; since the other side is not greener, it makes no sense to Tamplin that they should move together into an uncertain future. Tamplin is himself more cautious. Next, a shepherd appears, "a credible David" in a space and time which "might as easily be Galilee as Oxfordshire" (9); he also crosses the road, rubs snow in his eyes to wake himself up, and then mouths an apology for the delay to Sara. The description of the shepherd suggests something magical: an awakening not from ordinary sleep, but from myth. And this explains why Tamplin is so devastated by the shepherd's choice of Sara. Art and nature, continuous in this boy who "staged his grace as natural as breath," flow more readily to Sara than to Tamplin. Like the shepherd, she is capable of growth and motion. Tamplin sees a door opening for Sara, access to happiness through others since he has failed them both, and he "shift[s] gear quietly" (10). He accepts the "crushing, stifling but just and most beautiful" tale that it will be his fate to recount: he will "describe, celebrate, adore at a distance" (11) the happiness of others.

"A Dog's Death"

Following the departure of Sara's ship for America, Tamplin drives recklessly home and buries himself in sleep, "alone but not lonely" (12). His landlady wakes him with an urgent request, that Tamplin should serve as witness to her dog's death. The separation that the landlady faces is overtly linked to Tamplin's separation from Sara, and we have seen in the last story his willingness to preside over those death throes as well. He welcomes this new task, for it will test his capacity for distance. New rules operate in this first day without Sara: he must avoid contact, and so presses himself against the wall to avoid his landlady's touch. Tamplin's rules are "cold as glass" (15), recalling how a car window or aesthetic frame had insulated Tamplin (but not Sara) from the shepherd's greeting. Tamplin's concern with ritual is reflected by the veterinarian, who defends her own action by claiming that the dog's death is beautiful. An unpleasant reaching for sensation apparent in the first story, a tendency to write scenarios and focus on one's own responses, continues here. Tamplin postpones the kill so that he can come closer—to test himself, not to protect another creature. Now that the dog is dead, the rules allow Tamplin to touch it. As the dog's body and throat were " 'chocked with tumors' " (14), so now the contagion seems to spread to Tamplin. His throat is "crammed with knowledge that now was the time" to murder his love for Sara, but Tamplin is "powerless" (16) to do himself that kindness.

"Scars"

"Scars" describes a day some three weeks later. The threat of love's malignant survival has receded, and Tamplin seems firmly established in his "new self-sufficient life." He is asleep, "naked but alone, unthreatened, leaned on" only by the sun, which is "a quiet unneedful companion" (17)—unlike Sara, who in the first story had been "*on* him," implying "needs to face" (8). His sleep is like a child's, recalling Cary with his face "vapid as a baby's"; and he dreams of solitude, "of seeing through clear eyes an entire world less free than himself, hostages given by all but him" (18). Tamplin seems, then, not to be adoring from a distance (as promised in "The Happiness of Others"), but to be congratulating himself on immunity—his refusal to cross the road. The room in which he lives and works has formed around him "like a reef" and seems "sufficient fort against all but death" (17).

The shield is not perfect, however, for Tamplin is invaded by his landlady and her friend Mary, who tease him (threatening literal and figurative exposure) while Tamplin is dressed only in a towel. In a panic, he strikes Mary across the face and inflames an old scar. The violence of the act hurls Tamplin into a place where he and Mary seem the "only two ever alive and eternal; he brute, she victim." The experience of guilt is "his familiar home and his prison," a moment of déjà vu in which "he saw of course his mother's face [and] Sara his love's" (19) in Mary. Thus Price suggests that Tamplin's failure with Sara stems from an earlier failure related to his mother.

The sombre tone fades with the introduction of a banana-phallus and a string of related sexual jokes. Tamplin offers Mary the dildo upon her request, but she leaves it with him—implying that in his solitude he needs it more, and preferring herself to take " 'chances in the cruel world' " (23) of living persons. Mary declares " 'I'm *having* my life,' " (21) suggesting that she is aware of all the risks and opportunities involved; and she questions the life that Tamplin has chosen in limiting himself to the room and his work. Mary reveals to Tamplin the secret of his room, the fact that in all his treasured pictures and artifacts " 'No one's touching anyone.' " Intuitively, for

she lacks the required Japanese, Mary translates the inscription on
Tamplin's carving: " 'Hold-Me-Not' " (23), she says, and describes
that as her motto. Tamplin accepts this as his own motto as well and
promises Mary that he will be better dressed for their next meeting;
but she replies, " 'I've not even *seen* you, you're dressed so thick' "
(24).

Later, Tamplin's landlady tells him Mary's story. Mary's self-reli-
ance, we discover, differs from Tamplin's in that she engages rather
than rejects " 'the cruel world.' " She revolts against her husband's
mild demands, and ultimately against those of her father, and like
Tamplin she seeks " 'new life' " (33) and a " 'new chance' " (38);
but it does not occur to Mary to seek her chance in solitude. With
"sustained exhilaration of loathing" (34) Tamplin records this tale
called "Scars" for future use. His disgust with the chaos of Mary's
life, her pursuit of future pain, her insistent sexuality, makes Tamplin
seem repellently fastidious; his willingness to use her tale unsym-
pathetically seems parasitic.

Again, in the following scene, Tamplin's retreat into sleep is interrupted by the exigency of others. Mary enters his room and stands
over his bed like the minotaur in his Picasso etching, "above his vulnerable body, poised unseen for an unknown purpose" (36). Sug-
gestive of the role reversal implicit in his relationship to Mary, this
tableau casts Tamplin as Picasso's sleeping woman. While for Picasso
it was unclear whether the minotaur intended to kill or make love
to the woman, for Tamplin these alternatives merge. The fear he
experiences revives the faces of his previous vision, "each, judge and
victim" (36)—so that we understand that Tamplin's offense has always been the distrust of love. Mary has come because she needs a
place in which to make love with the man who is waiting for her
outside. Tamplin is appalled by the request; he imagines that his
chaste room is "stinking as though her hand had blindly sown stain,
as though he must scrape it all, scour it with acid before he could rest
again" (38). And he denies the favor which Mary has asked.

When Mary leaves, his room still feels infected by "the lethal illusion of contingency"; but Tamplin abjures flight, remembering that
"work was his journey; work his home—in the midst of whatever"
(39). In a sketch called "Seeds" he describes how a friend's mother
had told him the story of losing her husband in wartime. She was
self-contained and broke down only when her son came in and
exactly duplicated his father's bow. Tamplin supposes that the point

of his story resides in a genetic fate, the seed which necessarily flowers in a subsequent generation—a theme that is familiar in Price. But Tamplin will revise this interpretation after his final encounter with Mary, to decide that the title of "all stories was Scars not Seeds." The vulnerability of David's mother is the real issue of the tale and takes us closer to the heart of Price's fiction.

Possibly because of Tamplin's refusal, Mary has abandoned husband and father to go off with her new lover. Propelled by guilt, Tamplin goes in search of Mary to inform her of her father's imminent death. The message delivered, Tamplin realizes his powerlessness to "change another life," for Mary continues on her path unmoved, persistent. All stories are called "Scars," Tamplin realizes, because human beings *"rightly"* pursue courses that lead to pain through an involvement with other people. Only Tamplin protects himself in a life story called "Flight." Because Mary will not wait for her new life to begin, she leaves as a "gift" to Tamplin the ticket that he has earned for parking in a "NO WAITING" zone. While others pursue their lives, Tamplin waits—illegally, violating the most basic law of human society. Again, as in "The Happiness of Others," Tamplin "envied them all. For this moment, he worshiped their wasteful courage, ruinous choices, contingency" (50). The difference is that now Tamplin seems to recognize that his envy will be intermittent and that his own choice has been determined largely by fear.

"Waiting at Dachau"

This final episode of "Fool's Education" is the strongest piece of writing in *Permanent Errors*. Its action precedes and explains that of the other stories; but "Waiting at Dachau" is also a sequel because it is a retrospective narrative, offered by Tamplin as his "version" (52) of the summer vacation that he and Sara spent traveling through Scandinavia and Germany in 1957. The intended reader, Sara, is presented with the story's apparently central question on the first page: "Why did you balk and refuse to enter Dachau?" (51). Ultimately, however, it is with Tamplin's behavior and motives that we are concerned. In particular, we must assess the degree of self-criticism in his narrative, for the resolution depends on whether author, narrator, and reader can agree on the extent of the fool's education. Possibly we (and Sara) will refuse Tamplin the diploma he requests and that Price seems willing to issue.

If Tamplin and Sara "could enter Dachau together, face and com-
prehend its threat and still walk out together," they would be guaran-
teed "love not soluble in time or death . . . a perfect weld-job" (66).
That was Tamplin's plan, the test he explained to Sara in advance;
she, however, did not promise to comply—perhaps because she doubted
Tamplin's purpose, or because she disliked its theatricality. The camp
itself is a personal symbol for Tamplin, of hostility to love: he says
they are "exact contemporaries," that he is "one month older than
it and still running" (51). Running, of course, here means functioning; but the Tamplin whose life story was called "Flight," who ran
from a mass grave in "The Happiness of Others," is obviously "still
running" in another sense as well. He is also still functioning as a
death camp, as the purveyor of tragic endings. If Tamplin is Dachau,
his intention in entering the camp with Sara would surely be sus-
pect; his wish might be to confirm, rather than to deny, his later assertion that we all "in secret glee" want ultimately "to abandon all
human contracts" (84), to stand ruthlessly free. To take Sara into
Dachau's camp, through a town that ominously recalls the atmosphere
of his own childhood, would be to take her into the heart of his own
maze—to exorcise his past failures, his distrust of love, or to kill her
metaphorically. It is little wonder that Sara thinks Tamplin may not
be " 'safe to follow' " (82).

Tamplin's assessment of the meaning of Dachau is shockingly so-
lipsistic, although we may be persuaded by his line of vision because
it seems so painfully honest. Indeed, the whole of his reconstruction
has an objective quality—as if Tamplin were a careful witness in
some trial, admitting areas of doubt, sifting the evidence of photographs and historical detail. Tamplin ignores the obvious villains and
turns his righteous anger upon the victims, suggesting that they can
never be forgiven for betrayals of one another, and he implies that
all in varying degrees were guilty of this offense, even the de Wieks
whom he had first proposed as saints of love. His accusation is hor-
rible. It moves us because we recognize solitude as one truth of the
human condition, because it allows us to share in the guilt of the
holocaust, and because we see that Tamplin is speaking from some
deep, personal necessity.

To begin with, Tamplin casts Sara (because of her refusal to enter
Dachau with him) as one of those who cannot be forgiven for betrayal of a loved one; he casts himself as one who might have survived the test. Thus in the early pages of the story he is concerned

with establishing his love for Sara and with suggesting that even before Dachau she had begun to move away from him. He suggests that he cherished Sara, that he really *"saw"* (55) her; and he describes the day of their lunch by a Norwegian lake as *"The happiest day in all my life"* (54). This occasion, however, is now subjected to a peculiar analysis. Tamplin retains a photograph of Sara offering him some food, and he recalls Sara's having obliged him to move forward to get it. He wonders if he had required her to stage the gesture of service so that he could record it—and blames her for that compliance. He is embarrassed by this evidence of his own theatricality or his removal from the immediate present of the scene and feels that Sara should somehow have prevented it. He interprets her refusal to meet his eyes in the photograph as the beginning of her decision to abandon him. We recognize, however, that this "refusal" could be nothing at all, or only awkwardness; Tamplin's accusatory response is determined by his own sense of guilt, the chance that Sara had understood his theatrical manipulation of their time together. Also at issue in this scene is the question of equality: Tamplin would like to believe that this was not a problem in their relationship, or that Sara made it one unnecessarily. The evidence of the photograph makes Tamplin uncomfortable, however, so that he lashes out at Sara.

He next assesses their time in bed together, the miraculous achievement of "a perfect compound." But he goes on to question that, wondering if Sara were "merely drumming time through all [his] happy hours of artful plunging." He approves her thanking him afterwards, an action which sets Sara apart from all the less liberated, guilty maidens of Tamplin's experience. But she thanked him too perfunctorily, as though he "had zipped the back of [her] dress" (55). Whereas he would be drowned in gratitude and wakeful bliss, Sara was callous enough to crack jokes and fall asleep after lovemaking. In particular, he recalls the night before Dachau on which he had made love to Sara against her will; he blames her for not having absolved him utterly of the guilt that he experienced on that occasion. As with the lake scene, Tamplin expects Sara to protect him from embarrassment; her task is to enter fully into his conception of each occasion and never to imply that his sense of the occasion is excessive or in any way askew.

Shortly before arriving at Dachau, Tamplin offers to retract his plan; he is willing "to wait, stop short of the camp," believing that their relationship requires "no further *pro forma* buffeting" (58). Presumably this hesitation comes from his fear of losing Sara, now that the event is at hand which (as he later recognizes) was engineered to accomplish that separation. It has the added advantage of making it possible for Tamplin to blame Sara for urging them on. No longer seen as passive in the damage that she wreaks upon their love, Sara is now described as an Ariadne who "calmly leads dumb Theseus back into the lethal heart of the maze, its small tidy utterly efficient death chamber." This figure implies that Sara knows the identity of that "patient minotaur," the monster of solitude which is waiting to consume Tamplin; because she plans not to enter with him, Sara has withdrawn the life-line, Ariadne's thread. We cannot know, in fact, without Sara's "version," when she decided not to enter Dachau; in any case, Tamplin's sense of persecution seems unwarranted. The itinerary was his, and the monster lurking in Dachau was designed by him, for his own delectation.

On arriving at Dachau, Tamplin leaves the car unlocked—Sara wonders now if he had "started guessing [she] would stay behind?—guessing and hoping?" (59). If he had hoped Sara would abandon him, what are we to make of Tamplin's professed total submergence in his love? In truth, Tamplin appears uneasy before the strength of Sara's character, a strength which undermines his rather morbid romanticism. Sara also is an artist, but he easily discounts her "chaste tight painting" and assumes that after marriage they would "sail home to all the books [he'd] write"—books which he defines as "dreams of extracting love from [his] past, the boneyard of [his] childhood" (53). No mention is made of Sara's work or dreams. And the "boneyard" image is ominous, too closely linked to Dachau; Tamplin's dreams of love, in short, seem dangerously grounded upon the spectacle of failure, and they have too little to do with Sara herself. He interprets Sara's refusal to enter the camp as offering a "metaphor" of her own: "we'd be hitched to one load but in separate yokes" (70). That image of the married state is distasteful to him, and he rejects Sara's bid for independence because what Tamplin wants (if he wants Sara at all) is a clear understanding that he will define their one load, their single yoke. Thus Sara refuses to enter Dachau not because she wishes to harm Tamplin or to end their relationship, but because she is unwilling to accept his exclusive definition of their life together. Moreover, she is fearful of that definition and of Tamplin's possible wish to destroy their love; and she dislikes his unhealthy, obsessive melodrama.

Tamplin enters Dachau alone, and the experience is largely anti-climactic. Because (as he thinks at first) Dachau inherently lacks "the mystery of place" (64), he is not deeply affected by the experience. Tamplin offers comparisons with other shrines to human evil in which the mystery was still potent—all of which are associated with intensely narcissistic historical figures, a fact which is underscored by the presence in Nero's palace of "an elderly English gentleman masturbating." He cites, too, the reliquary of Christ's manger in Santa Maria Maggiore, which he says appeared "as immanent with promise and threat to my life as a gram of radium bombarding my eyes." In contrast to the other examples, Christ offers the model of selfless love which is perceived in part as a "threat" by Tamplin because of his narcissistic tendencies. In all of these cases the mystery of place seems to have survived because of some relevance to Tamplin's own experience. He finally concludes that Dachau lacked this power because he had "expected *home*" (65). That expectation was revealed by what Tamplin now recognizes as his mistaken sense that the environs of Dachau resembled eastern North Carolina; the camp itself failed to live up to that expectation because Sara refused to go in with him, declined this chance to return to his "birthplace," and so to attempt with him the resurrection of love from its "boneyard."

Following the visit to Dachau, Tamplin sinks deeper into the trap he has built for himself. He had dismissed Sara as "half-sadist, half-coward" (68), but is "not prepared to abandon [her] physically" (69)—as he is several times tempted to do in this story and in "The Happiness of Others." When Sara sings the reconcilation ensemble from *Figaro*, which they will hear that night in Salzburg, Tamplin is infuriated by its implicit suggestion that she should be the one to forgive him. " 'Why in all your extensive *reconciliation* repertoire,' " he asks, " 'is it always the *lady* dispensing largess?' " (70). The answer, for each example he gives, is that the man is at fault—a point which escapes Tamplin, however. Looking back on this phase of their journey, Tamplin finds that his memory of it is imperfect. "You've greased my hands," he tells Sara, but displays familiar uncertainty about her active part in his fate when he adds "or is it only some new lubricant...manufactured now in me?" Related to this protective, distancing "lubricant" is Tamplin's suggestion that he and Sara had become "a team of cut-rate Midases, transmuting all [they] touched to chalk." Thus at Mozart's birthplace Sara disrespectfully, audaciously, signs the guest-book *"Veronica F. Pertle and traveling companion"* (71), and at the opera itself Tamplin falls asleep.

In the restaurant afterwards they are accosted by gypsies. Tamplin requires Sara to have her picture taken while holding a sleepy lion cub, offered to her with its "paws together in a mockery of prayer (its high testicles were pink as salmon, utterly vulnerable)." The tableau of Sara and the lion cub unmistakably suggests both the madonna and child and the relationship of Sara and Tamplin. Wearing a dress through which "much white skin showed," Sara allows the lion to be hung on her shoulder "like a child" (74). The cub fastens its teeth in her shoulder, but Sara reacts calmly and with control. As she strokes and talks the lion free from its grip, Tamplin wonders "What nourishment was he taking?—what pleasure, fulfillment?" (75). Tamplin's sexual vulnerability, his parasitic relationship to Sara, and his complex and usually hidden concern with his own mother are all contained and associated by this tableau. The lion cub has lost its mother, and Sara's suggestion that the mother lion was killed combines with the cub's attack upon Sara to reveal Tamplin's sense of betrayal by and of his own mother, for whom Sara is a substitute.

Engrossed in his dessert, Tamplin ridiculously defends his ability to "sit for whole half-hours, thinking nothing" (76) while Sara tends to her own wound in the washroom. He is "an engine geared for one purpose—the expulsion of waste parts, self-starting restored" (77). On the proprietor's insistence, Tamplin eventually follows Sara, but even as he looks back on that scene, he seeks to blame Sara for his distance—"Weren't you throwing off a field of volts that I'd never have pierced, however determined?" (78). Sara's response, when Tamplin answers " 'Good' " to her statement that she has sustained only " 'one canine puncture,' " reveals that she has suffered from his evasion and his wish to hurt her: " 'Yes, *marvelous.* Something *in* me finally. And a permanent mark' " (78).

Jesus re-enters the story at this point. A "promise and threat" (65) to Tamplin, Christ has been summoned by Sara in her need. On the bathroom mirror she has written, *"Jesus, will you help me now? I will. I have."* At first, Tamplin considers whether the message was theatrically intended for him or written in imitation of J. D. Salinger's *Franny,* but he decides that something more serious is at work—that Sara has enlisted some "new fierce power" (79) in her service. Christ has helped Sara to endure her trial with the lion cub and will help her again in the scene that follows where Sara (perhaps remembering the humility that led Christ to forgive His murderers) finds the strength to ask pardon for the injustice Tamplin feels she has dealt him. Perhaps Christ also gave her the sight of Andromeda, the galaxy which is later described as "the sort of gift that God the Father might have willed for the Infant Christ" (86), a photograph of which Tamplin later strategically hangs "only just below" (85) his Rembrandt print of Jesus. But Tamplin is unimpressed by Sara's wish to show him Andromeda; he adopts a familiar posture of superiority and judges her performance as "way below standard" (81). Moreover, he rejects her graceful apology. Milking this pathetic moment, suppressing an instinct to accept her offer of renewed love, he asks Sara to " 'Give [him] time' " (82).

Although Tamplin yearns for a repeat performance of this scene, Sara never gives it to him. He cannot, apparently, forgive her of his own volition; she must beg. "You never asked again," he tells her mournfully, and skillfully redirects the blame to her: "Your silence and patience only fueled my flight, stoked a natural warmth of sadism in me" (83). Recalling the transmutation of gold to chalk and the "lubricant" which had been produced following the failure at Dachau, "a glaze of scum . . . self-surrendered vandalism" pours across "all those Rembrandts and Vermeers that might have saved" him. Neither great art nor Sara's continued presence is allowed to redeem Tamplin from his self-absorption; he prefers to masturbate like the English gentleman, to decide that after all it was his deepest wish to sever all ties with love, to fly away from her "at stunning speeds like [Sara's] galaxy" (83).

In the final pages of the story Tamplin discusses the Andromeda galaxy which Sara had shown him on the night she asked for pardon. On that occasion he had seen it as "a faint smear, an old chalk fingerprint" (80); and his failure to grant Andromeda its full meaning and beauty casts Tamplin again as a Midas in reverse, turning gold to chalk. Now he questions whether that was in fact Andromeda; still typically, he thinks Sara might have been lying for effect. But he decides to grant Sara's honesty, and furthermore to articulate for her the meaning of Andromeda, to supply the poem she was "always aching to write." Tamplin's ego is still firmly in place, as he reminds Sara that his poem "would be better but that's [his] job, right?" (86). Andromeda is in flight, Tamplin says, not (as he was) from love itself, but from *"two repellent objects at the core of space"*—the failure of his affair with Sara. *"Less narcissistically"* (87), he allows that Andromeda flees from all human failures in love. Echoing Sara's assertion that her reconciliation repertoire reflects "'the way the world's built'" (70), Tamplin states that a desire for union *"is how the world is made."* He has come around to the position espoused by Sara's favored epitaph in the first story and to an acceptance of Christ's commandment that we must love one another. He ends the story by telling Sara that there are "no options," that "God only watches comedies," and he issues a last request: "Sara, come back" (87). He is ready to forgive her and perhaps to apologize for the long delay, but there is little evidence that Tamplin has relinquished enough of his pride to make room for Sara in his life or to understand her behavior at Dachau. She might do well not to comply.

"Elegies"

In "Elegies" Price turns his attention to the deaths of his parents ("Late Warnings"), of a writing friend ("Invitation, for Jessie Rehder"), and of his own innocence in childhood ("Summer Games"). We are aware of deep connections throughout the book and are accustomed to a discontinuous mode of narration, so that the autobiographical note struck by "Elegies" seems to reverberate throughout the whole. The photograph of the author's parents and his "sifting the debris of [his] mother's death" (99) in "Late Warnings" are familiar from *Love and Work*; thus we associate Price to some degree with Eborn and with the various male protagonists who resemble Eborn. The difficulty that Eborn has with his marriage, his fear of contingency, and his identity as artist seem to be played out in the rest of *Permanent Errors*, while "Late Warnings" asserts the essential role of the parents in the psychodrama of the whole.

"Elegies" as a whole enforces our recognition that throughout *Permanent Errors* love is examined within the context of death. The threat of death is felt as a motive for human love, which in turn is threatened by death in several ways. Our vulnerability to death is increased if we love others, for they become "hostages" (18) to fate; but if that fear causes us to retreat from love, our best defense against death's sting may be lost. If our task as human beings is to love one another, then death becomes an enemy in another sense: it may descend at any moment, before love's failures have been repaired. We can be left with permanent errors on our hands. Still more frightening is the possibility that we are attracted by death's power to sever human ties and to reveal our ultimate solitude.

In "Late Warnings" Price meditates upon the photograph of his parents, which on the cover of *Permanent Errors* is superimposed upon a drawing of a Chinese symbol for unity, the cohesion of Yin and Yang (the male and female principles). His mother's hip is thrust out in a curve against his father's body to echo that design. But Price is troubled by the photograph, despite evidence that his parents were successfully joined: he asks "Why does their shadow not resemble them?" and notes that his father's leg is obscured, as if these peculiarities were evidence of mutability. He wants them to *"take shelter in time,"* and then asks "shelter from what?" (92). What we sense here is Price's own uncertainty: is love eternally triumphant, or is death? Premonitions of death (familiar from "Scars" and *Love and Work*) are seen as futile, since he "could still not save [his] love from death" (98).

In the tender Jessie Rehder elegy Price again suggests that we live in the shadow of death. Jessie knew that: she kept a "medieval Dance of Death" (106) in which she saw the likeness of herself dancing with two skeletons and a mysterious young man. The acknowledged pain of Jessie's life is seen as her solitary state, imaged by the fact that the young man is anonymous, unrealized; still she dances, "free *and* sentenced" (105) to death, and keeps her eyes clean—as does Price, her friend. The final elegy is only loosely that, but is the darkest of all: it describes how Price as a child playing at war games discovered that death is not purely an external threat. There is something murderous in human beings, he says, something "which sets us wild against ourselves ... [and] worst of all our love" (111).

"Truth and Lies"

Set in eastern North Carolina, "Truth and Lies" (the first part of "Home Life") offers another variation on the book's theme: this time a female protagonist, as unreliable as Tamplin in her presentation of self and history, is assigned Eborn's "hole in the heart" and finds that her life is " '*stopped*' " (134) by error. Sarah Wilson is married to Nathan, one of the author's unhappy, alcoholic buccaneers, and is herself miserable. In her husband's pocket Sarah finds proof of his most recent infidelity and decides to take Nathan's place in a rendezvous with Ella. When Sarah first sees the girl she appears "giant,"

but we are told "she shrank as she came" until she "reached her
natural size" (115). So it seems that this obstacle to the continuation
of Sarah's pitiful marriage can be dealt with after all—that Ella is
" 'nothing but an ignorant child' " her husband has " 'tinkered with' "
(118). By the end of the story, however, we recognize that Ella's
strength is superior to Sarah's: "whatever her debts, she owned herself." Ella is "free" (133), as Sarah is not—in part because she has
escaped from childhood without that painfully unresolved relationship to her father that spelled Sarah's doom. Ella is fertile; she can
go on, that is, to the work of the next generation. But Sarah is locked
in the sterility of the past.

Like Tamplin, Sarah relies on facility with speech. She anticipates,
in questioning Ella, responses that match her own dramatic conception of the affair; but the truth she receives from Ella deflates her,
revealing Ella's dignity (like Sara's in "Fool's Education") and her
more natural approach to life. At first the drive that the two women
take is intended merely as an occasion for talk. Sarah realizes, however, that mere confrontation may not suffice to end the affair, so she
takes advantage of the direction in which her car has ominously
traveled—to Kinley, the site of her childhood. She decides to tell her
story, a pitiable tale which will prove to Ella that she has the right
at least to keep her own husband.

Although the lie that Sarah later tells Ella may cause us to distrust her tale, probably Sarah's only distortions are interpretive. Most
noticeable is her sense of betrayal, centering on the house that her
father sold to fund her education. Though Sarah indicates that her
relationship to both parents was happy and that she wishes only to
" 'make as good a life as [her] parents had had,' " we begin to
doubt that Sarah felt herself sufficiently included in the family's happiness. We are told, for instance, that she would ask her mother for
" 'brothers, company' " and that her mother would reply " 'Sarah, I
thought we were happy. Why aren't you satisfied?' " (125). Her
mother eventually dies from trying to fulfill Sarah's wish for siblings,
and Sarah's unacknowledged sense of guilt, revealed by her feeling
that she " 'must have looked bad—dirty and torn,' " contributes to our
growing sense that Sarah misconceives her past. Significantly, she believes that the three years after her mother's death " 'were the happiest' " simply because she does not remember them: " 'I have never
forgotten one painful thing.' " But she also questions whether her
father felt as she did, that father and daughter " 'were sufficient to

one another and would go on being'" (126). She is like Tamplin, who "dreams of extracting love from . . . the boneyard of [his] childhood" (53). And the house of love becomes for Sarah, as it does for Eborn, an emblem of dispossession. Like Eborn, she is incapable of moving on (as her father had hoped she would) to a mature life of her own.

At the beginning of the story we are told that Sarah has a "hole at the core of her chest" (115). This hole is understood as a sensation indicative of fear, but Price develops a chain of hole images suggesting that the hole is related to Sarah's immaturity: an unassuaged pain makes it impossible for her to go forward with her life. Ella's sister's failure to produce a living child affected her heart, and Sarah's mother's heart was "'poisoned'" (125) in the same way. But Sarah's sterility, associated with the hole in her heart, is emblematic of something larger: the arrested development that had destroyed Sarah's marriage, despite her attempt at "'healing wounds'" (129). Nathan also needs someone to "'plug up his chest'" (130), to release him from the guilt that he feels for his past; but Sarah has failed in that because of her own exaggerated grievances and because her failure to give Nathan a child (or a real marriage) has led him to continue with his self-destructive drinking. Probably she does not know who is responsible for their childlessness, but she lies to Ella—describing the sterility she imputes to Nathan as "'one more hole through the middle of him'" (131). That lie rebounds, however, when Ella reveals that she has just aborted Nathan's child.

Sarah's guilt stems from her own rapacious need for love and the willingness to blame others for her own lack. The permanent error that she commits with the lie stands for that larger error, which began long ago. Her journey into the past with Ella, through desolate country and into the heart of her tale, serves ironically to reveal Sarah as one who demanded more than she was able to give. She begins the story with a sense of herself as a victimized avenger, set to spring upon Ella as the rabbit with its "eye congealed in terror" (115). And she thinks for a while that she has triumphed over Ella with her lie. But Sarah ends as her own prey, when her car (the engine of a self-destructive journey into the past) strikes another rabbit, and she feels in the "fine bones" of her hands on the wheel "its brittle death." Sarah has finally become aware that it was she who "*stopped*'" (134) her life with Nathan.

"Good and Bad Dreams"

The second part of "Home Life" provides an even more harrowing look at the domestic scene, in which suicide comes into focus as both a permanent error and a response to the male protagonist's permanent failure in love. The question of Lucas's culpability in his wife's suicide attempt is the central issue in the six fragmentary scenes of "Good and Bad Dreams." Our first sight is of Lucas alone, at home on "his first free solitary day in months" (135), and the elation he feels suggests that the forced intimacy of marriage is abhorrent to him. Lucas occupies as much as he can a separate world, but even to breathe the same air as his wife seems a painful compromise and a restriction of his freedom: alone, Lucas can adjust the temperature of the room to suit his own taste exactly. He can indulge in fears he would hide from his wife and take jubilant pleasure in his own body.

His day is interrupted when he sees a dying bat in the backyard. At first he attempts to ignore it, to retreat into his own space. Later, he decides to dispatch and bury the animal which he fears; and suddenly he understands that the bat is "messenger, sign" (140), of his wife's approaching suicide. As he kills the bat, so effectively does Lucas speed his wife's death. The bat is a parasite or vampire; and Lucas sees his marriage, "his promise to her," as having "sapped" (137) every day of his life for years, just as the bat had "hogged his day" (139). Alone and naked in his room, Lucas peers through his legs to see that his "dangling sex" has "transfixed the unmade bed— stake in the heart of the vampire" (135). The bed as symbol of their sexual union is for Lucas a symbol of his wife's debilitating and parasitical attachment to him; but the image permits us to see also that it is the peculiar nature of Lucas's sexuality that thrusts the stake in her heart. In a later scene she appears as "a mouth on his helpless chest, dull-toothed, draining" (147). Standing before the bat, Lucas feels "vulnerable, precisely in his eyes and throat" (137), as Tamplin had when beckoned by Sara to witness the Andromeda galaxy. Eborn too feels threatened by women attached to him as mouths "to his throat, toothless, warm."[3] (The line between mother and sexual partner, revealing each woman as victim and judge of the male protagonist, continues from Love and Work and "Fool's Education" in the glimpse that Lucas has of his mother's death in his wife's dreaming face.) All three men feel a need to "grow [their] own rind" (139), to flee the demands of contingency; and all three are uncomfortable with sexual union, better able to deal with their erotic impulses by solitude. Lucas attempts narcissistically to kiss his own penis and then his mirrored lips, believing that they "could use the greeting" (136); the neglect he feels stems not from a dearth of opportunity to employ his wife's "facilities," but from a wish to make love to himself in blessed solitude. Sexually, Lucas feels that he belongs "to another species with analogous parts but incomprehensible needs"; in making love to his wife, he is like "the priest of a heresy who entered to perform his rite on her altar," obtaining finally a "reward" that is "sealed from her" (141). The heresy, it would seem, is not Lucas's masculinity on a feminine altar, but his onanism.

The description of the suicide attempt is chilling, offered by an anonymous narrative voice; behind that, however, we sense both Lucas and his wife taking some final, gruesome satisfaction in the details of the scene. Like Tamplin with Dachau and the dog, or Eborn with the deaths of his mother and the boy on the highway, Lucas attempts to contain and defuse the threat of his own complicity by clinical analysis. He cannot, however, rid himself of guilt. Having earlier seen himself as Rilke's "archaic Apollo," issuing the familiar edict *"You must change your life"* (136), and wishing to change in the direction of greater solitude, Lucas is now faced with the need to achieve greater intimacy with his wife. He must forestall a second attempt at suicide, but cannot even ask her motive for the first. Only when his wife is asleep can he extract the fact of his guilt; and in these still appallingly distant circumstances, his "pitiful humping amends" (150) cannot suffice to save her. In one dream his wife appears as vampire-angel come to judge and kill him; Lucas makes himself vulnerable to her, while she draws forth "speech not blood, one word 'Pardon'" (153). In a subsequent dream vision, when Lucas would "rush to save her," his "heart refuses" (154). Pardon cannot be granted, Christ in another dream cannot find the water he needs to wash Lucas's feet in forgiveness, and so must use His scalding spit, because Lucas cannot genuinely wish to save his wife.

"Walking Lessons"

"Walking Lessons" is the single entry in the book's final section, which is called "The Alchemist" because of the dark aesthetic powers displayed by the writer-protagonist. The unnamed narrator has arrived in Arizona to visit his friend Blix, a VISTA volunteer with the Navaho, and to avoid Christmas at home: his wife has committed suicide two weeks before. The pace of his tale is leisurely because the narrator's goal is to delay confrontation with the question of his wife's death. He labors, for example, to order the chaos of Blix's quarters so that the "contagion" he senses there cannot force his head "to acknowledge its own mess" (168). Yet he is aware of the sensational figure he must seem to others as the mate of a suicide, and exploits this shamelessly in his dealings with Neely, the VISTA agent, and Dora, his friend's Navaho mistress. Inexorably, the story moves its narrator into precisely the psychological landscape he requires and had wished to escape.

It is tempting to view "Walking Lessons" as a sequel to "Good and Bad Dreams." It seems, for example, that Price is mirroring the two stories by withholding in each the name of one of the partners and by assigning mystical importance to the single occasion in each story where he does reveal a name—Lucas or Beth. The narrator's peculiar assertion that Beth might have intended only to warn him with an attempted suicide, although her method was a fail-safe pistol in the mouth, can be explained if we decide that indeed he is Lucas and that he cannot admit to his wife's previous attempt. It would be a mistake, however, to insist upon this equation. Price encourages us to detect resemblances throughout *Permanent Errors* and also establishes the autonomy of each story in order to make an important point about the artistic process. The alchemist's glory and his ordeal are to perform the feat of transformation again and again, but each time differently; each fresh try involves infinite, subtle variations upon his single basic experiment.

One obvious change as we move from "Good and Bad Dreams" to "Walking Lessons," from an attempted to a successful suicide, is the narrator's anger at his wife for leaving him "dumb with guilt and mystery, unable to answer the final indictment flung at the living by a suicide" (171). The enormity of his wife's crime, her refusal to grant him fair trial, threatens to distract the narrator from his necessary task of self-indictment and eventual self-forgiveness. We do not see and he does not analyze the marriage. In place of Lucas's response to his wife's proximity, however, we have the narrator's response to the ideal of contingency as exemplified by Blix; and so we are prepared for the narrator's discovery that he has in part willed Beth's suicide for the sake of his solitude.

Blix is a foil for the narrator's emphasis on self-preservation, personal survival. His motive in coming to Arizona is antithetical to the narrator's; an ex-medical student, Blix has come to help the Navajo, not to appreciate the possibility that he is more fortunate than they. He has learned that the sense of guilt with which he began is essentially onanistic and has progressed from " 'self-service' " (162), a euphemism for masturbation, to a sexual relationship with Dora, which signals his active involvement with the fate of the Navajo. But Dora has just discovered that she is dying slowly of multiple sclerosis, and her condition becomes a metaphor (particularly in the narrator's mind) of the hopelessness of Blix's efforts to help other people. While Blix is aware of his own inefficacy, he persists in his charitable course—despite mockery and despite being tempted by the doctrine of solitary self-preservation which the narrator espouses. Doctors and lovers alike play a losing game: sooner or later, they are defeated by death. Ultimately, however, Blix recognizes that he cannot retire from love or service to others on that account.

The narrator's solitude is half chosen and half a belief that people have no choice but to be alone. The foreign world of the Navajo, where "interlingual misfires" (183) are a common occurrence, confirms for him the essential isolation of human beings. As Tamplin is "a fish in air" (50), however, so the narrator cannot " 'speak the language, can barely breathe the air' " (241) for reasons that may be peculiar to himself. Blix diagnoses the narrator's reaction to his wife's death as curable because " 'to be scraped . . . bare—owing nobody life, help' " is what he has always sought. Even sex, Blix suggests, was ultimately a separate and selfish experience for the narrator: " 'Did you ever *come* for her, ever donate that much?' "

Shaken by this accusation, and by the macabre suggestion that he take Dora as the " 'petrifying' " vessel of his next sexual donation, the narrator fears that Blix will "be converted, by his own life and the nearness of mine, to monstrosity" (189). The vision of the narrator as monster is sustained by references to him as " 'Mr. Scorch,' " in whose wake everything " '*stiffens*' " or " 'bleeds' " (196), as the " 'Prince of Darkness' " (205), as a "Halloween" (229) ghoul, and as " 'some kind of witch or something' " (224). When asked by the narrator what kind of monster he is, Blix replies " 'There's only one— the killing kind' " (223). The narrator's monstrosity is in his willingness to stand back and watch as others suffer. His vision is of a bleak world where a five-year-old "Polyneices with a plastic bow and arrow" strives eternally to kill his brother—and, we know from

Sophocles' *Antigone*, is in turn murdered by his brother; no reprieve
seems possible to the narrator, for these Navajo children are surrounded by "immortal American litter" (199). Blix and Dora, the
narrator believes, will become "two more litter factories" (239) in
this permanently blighted landscape. They will succumb to entropy
or the "second law of thermodynamics" (180), an inevitable loss of
heat: Dora's " 'warm hole' " is already " 'cooling' " (242). The question, of course, is whether the monstrous vision is the true one—or
whether the narrator, " 'Frozen—Birdseye Brains' " (222), simply
imposes his own chill on others.

The narrator's stance is that of the observer. Watching Dora, he
wishes "to be transparent . . . a witness clear as a pane of glass"
(221)—recalling Tamplin's glass barrier. His narration is punctuated
by attempts to frame his experience, to title it. He wonders "who
would be the ideal painter to paint us" (194), settling on Brueghel;
and for the spectacle of Indians toiling in the mud while he is safely
enclosed behind the truck's window, he offers as title "*The Drones
and the Mate.*" Seeing himself as "the consort chosen . . . and groomed
for union" (207), the narrator regards himself as infinitely precious,
deserving of all possible protection; the union toward which he is
aimed, however, is with his work rather than with other creatures.
His object in "Walking Lessons" is to come to terms with these two
conflicting images of himself, as monster and superior person. To do
this he must make himself vulnerable: he must face his role in Beth's
death and permit his superior suede shoes to be ruined in the common mud. He must walk for a time with people who seem to him
of another species altogether.

The journey to rescue Dora's truck, which he undertakes with Blix
and Dora and a motley crew of Navajos, supplies this opportunity.
His powers as an artist, linked to the dark forces which are assigned
to him by the Navajo as one pursued by his wife's ghost, metaphorically suffice to accomplish one miracle: safe behind glass at the
wheel of Blix's truck, he manages to extract the truck from the mud in
which it has been swamped. Blix then permits him to drive the truck,
and "piloting at last—not ideally, not alone . . . but at least at nobody's
mercy but [his] own" (210), the narrator feels reasonably safe. At
this stage of the journey the narrator has acknowledged his rage—his
wish to consign all suicides to the "*Ninth*" Circle" of Dante's hell as
" 'Traitors to Their Kin' " (171)—and has been prompted by Blix
to the recognition that he is " 'left alone because [he] wanted to

be' " (202), that he wants to be "free not to yield again to Love the Great Occupation, Time-Passer, Killer" (206). But he has not yet put those facts together. He can exorcise that rage and what he sees as his wife's vindictive try at spoiling the rest of his life if he sees that he has "foiled her death, her punishment by the simple expedient of desiring it, *requiring* it" (238). To achieve that perspective, however, he must first be seriously threatened with extinction. He must sink into the mud which threatens all in order to see how badly he wants to get on with his own life.

Blix describes himself as " 'fighting . . . not explaining human life' " (198); in his long, cold walk back to civilization, the narrator must do some fighting of his own. Still, the explanations persist. Justifying himself as writer, he asserts a preference for describing the psychological rather than the physical dimensions of his struggle for survival. But it is clear that the one comes into focus for him through the other. Previously, the narrator had thought he could escape the entropy which he sees as operative in the lives of Blix and Dora: through art, he "could radiate, steady and generous, for years without visible exhaustion—the radiance of simple knowledge . . . the wasteless conversion of mass into power" (207). With chill death a distinct possibility, he now sees himself as one of "three running-down lives in a running-down world" (236). Shared vulnerability leads him to a greater sympathy for others and an acceptance of their divergent paths when the threat of death recedes.

The physical dangers of cold and gunfire which the narrator must endure are parallel to the psychological exposure to his wife's chilly, hostile ghost; thus he acknowledges that the shot fired at his party by a defensive landowner is not " 'the first shot ever fired' " at him, but " 'the second' " (249). His reference, of course, is to his wife's suicidal shot, which he believes was aimed at him. But he discovers that this second shot is aimed at Dora (his wife's double), and this leads to his recognition that Beth committed suicide for reasons of her own which he can never entirely know. He is not the center of the universe, not the only cause of her death. Dora becomes Beth in the peculiar lunar landscape, the "Death Valley" (211), through which these travelers journey. Like Beth, she considers suicide: she asks the narrator to kill her, and we gather that she has also made this request of Blix. Both Dora and Blix, in the narrator's imagination, seem agents of Beth's desire for vengeance; he senses that this whole excursion has been staged to punish him. Beth is everywhere—in the watchful satellite above (an ironic version of the Star of Bethlehem) and in the humming of the electrical wires whose power is "scary and disembodied" (238), whose force is ended when the narrator grants the justice of his wife's complaint against him and begs her pardon through Dora.

As the story ends, we realize that the journey has had another meaning for Blix and Dora. Blix had asked the narrator's help, seeing him as one who had found the " 'way out' " (234) of contingency. The advice offered is that Blix may " 'never walk alone,' " but he " 'sure as Hell can *run*' " (236) from a love as doomed as that which Dora offers. Both Dora and Blix, however, opt for continuance: Dora chooses to live, and Blix chooses to accompany her for as long as her journey lasts. Their experience in "Death Valley" has led all three characters to value their lives and has confirmed them in solitude or the paired life, the two divergent paths which are possible to human beings. Death comes sooner or later, whichever route is taken. Dangers such as are imaged by Dora's disease or by Beth's ghost must be faced down; people must accept who and what they are; the goal is continuance, for however long it lasts. In the end the characters agree to differ. The narrator is happy, he tells Blix, because he has realized " 'There are people like me' "; and Blix replies, " 'So what . . . there are more like me' " (251). The phrase "so what" (173) is Beth's; it signals for the narrator an unanswerable difference between human beings, which he will not allow to stop him in his tracks. The last title that he assigns to their common venture is " *'Happy Though Breathing'* " (253). Breathing for different purposes, in adversity of different kinds, both sorts of people are finally happy to be alive.

Chapter Seven
The Surface of Earth

Introduction

The controversy that surrounds *The Surface of Earth* can be approached through Richard Gilman's inflammatory description of the book as a "mastodon," a "great lumbering archaic beast."[1] When that judgment appeared in *The New York Times Book Review*, Eudora Welty and others leapt to the defense of Reynolds Price and of Southern literature generally, with its emphasis upon the past and family ties.[2] Price was anachronistic, Gilman felt, in producing "a relentless family saga at a time when most of us feel self-generated inheritors of obliterated pasts." In fact, Price is concerned here with a tension between genetic or environmental fate and the possibility of something like self-generation; his people have roots, and search for them, and search also for ways of escaping what those roots entail.

Although not antediluvian, *The Surface of Earth* does seem a peculiar beast—particularly if we approach it as a strictly realistic novel, or if we somehow fail to recognize its symbolic dimension. The characters speak with an unnatural intensity about the guilt and longing in which all are enmeshed; and they sound remarkably alike. They talk endlessly about private feelings; in their numerous letters and dreams, those feelings are projected still more intensely. Past familial events, usually errors of some kind, are ceaselessly examined from a variety of perspectives and never entirely laid to rest, because these characters have a desperate faith in the utility of such knowledge for the understanding or amelioration of their own lives. Gilman is right to call this saga "relentless": nothing is casual or extraneous, and nothing dilutes the intensity which seems at once less natural than our own lives and more so. Not surprisingly, some reviewers have suggested that the novel would be improved by greater variety of tone or by substantial cuts—and they may be right; but it is also possible that *The Surface of Earth* would lose something of its fierce integrity in the process.

Referring to the "'unrealistic'" events that occur in *A Generous*

Man, Price argued that "the return of the dead, outrageous coincidence, great rushes of communication between people, great avowals of love or hate" are expressions of something that lies "only slightly beneath the surface of the world of most men."[3] In *The Surface of Earth* some features of the romance are muted—the holiday atmosphere is gone, and ghosts appear only in dreams. But Price is again concerned with an unseen world which can erupt and transfigure the surface of our daily lives. The unrealistic intensity of his characters suggests their longing for that world, their wish to break through to a center of meaning and rest. And this supplies the central metaphor of Price's novel: in all their traveling, waiting, talking, and dreaming, his people search the surface of earth for their center of rest. They travel mainly between Fontaine, North Carolina, and three places in Virginia—Richmond, Bracey, and Goshen. And their repetitive journeys recall the circular dirt road of *A Long and Happy Life*, beyond which Price strategically places the healing and killing springs of love. Nature waits for them, offering glimpses (points of entry) into the unseen world for which his people yearn, and which they will find at last in death. Their horizontal search from one place or person to another is a measure of frustration, for the proper direction of their journey is vertical and leads to the love of God.

The composition of *The Surface of Earth* has a long and complex history. It began, Price tells us, with the image of a boy (himself, or Hutch in the novel) traveling with an alcoholic father by car through eastern North Carolina. Both figures were yearning for love. To tell his story properly, Price found that he had to back up more than forty years—back through the father's promise to give up drink if wife and child survived the ordeal of childbirth, back still more into the family history which might explain the web of guilt and longing and impulse toward flight in which both father and son were entangled. The germ of his tale was dramatized in "The Names and Faces of Heroes," but to examine fully the attractions of love or contingency on the one hand, and solitude or freedom on the other, would require for Price a much more elaborate excavation of what Tamplin referred to as the "boneyard" of his past.

Book One: "Absolute Pleasures"

The opening scene of the novel has Bedford Kendal revealing to his children (Eva, Kennerly, and Rena) their quintessential family history—that their grandmother died in giving birth to their mother, and that their grandfather, believing he had killed his wife, then committed suicide. Their mother's life has been spoiled by this desertion and her own guilt; she has also been turned against sex as the appetite that kills, and Bedford has for many years honored her aversion. Harshly, the children define their mother and grandfather as killers; all three seem thoroughly attuned to this story's dire vision of the harm that family members can wreak upon one another. Into this scene of less-than-absolute pleasures comes Forrest Mayfield, a thirty-two-year-old Latin teacher who will elope that evening with Eva, his star pupil. Ironically, he tells Bedford " 'you've got all I ever wanted, here,' "[4] meaning not only Eva but the spectacle of a rooted, presumably happy family life. He then attacks that family by removing Eva, "the last bond that held [the Kendals] in harness" (27). This is a constant theme in the novel: any establishment of a new household damages a previous combination of human lives and may, therefore, be a mistake. Forrest and Eva, their names suggest, are a primal couple with fresh, new lives ahead. But that proves to be an illusion; family histories are too strong, and at least "ten lives," through several generations, are "bent crooked" (446) by their error.

Forrest's heart is dry and starved. He wants through Eva to escape the solitude that he suspects is his natural condition, and his excitement in the face of what seems a reprieve—the promise of absolute pleasures—is too much for Eva. His needs are too great, would leave his girl bride too little space for herself or her love of Bedford. Forrest's hunger is an inheritance from his father, revealed in a memory of Robinson Mayfield with needy eyes stretched full-length over the body of his son. On her wedding night, following an idyllic sexual experience, Eva has a vision of her own father's body extended on her in precisely that manner—a "vision of the ruin she had willed on her home" (10) by spurning Bedford; and she endures Forrest's second conjugal embrace as if he too were an incubus, but the wrong one. To the harsh Kendal sensibility in which Eva shares, there appears something weak and womanish in Forrest's kindliness. Because he clings to her, fearing Eva's attraction to her family, and because he lacks Robinson's cruel magnetism, the ability to compel love, Forrest begins to lose Eva.

Eva and the infant Rob nearly succumb to the rigors of childbirth which kill so many women (and children) in this book, and afflict

with guilt the husbands and children who survive. History threatens
to repeat itself at this point: Eva imagines that she is dying and asks
Forrest to stay, not to kill himself as her grandfather had done.
Before they are out of danger, the blow falls elsewhere—as Eva's
mother commits suicide to punish Eva for her carnality and to fulfill her own tragic destiny. Everyone blames Forrest and Eva for their
defection. Thorne Bradley blames Forrest, for whom apparently he
harbors a homosexual love. Rena and Kennerly blame Eva, but are
also darkly pleased by her betrayal since they hope it will increase
the portion of parental love that falls to them; their mother's death
increases that anger, confirming the damage that Eva has wrought.
And the chorus of abuse is triumphant: Eva leaves Bracey, where
she has lived with Forrest in his sister's house, to return with Rob
to her father's home in Fontaine. Eva realizes that she left in the
first place largely because of her mother, her sense that she was not
sufficiently cherished, and that now she must repay her father for
that rapacity which led to her mother's death: she can do so quite
happily now that the mother is gone. Periodically, Eva will reach
out again to Forrest. The love of her father, however, is greater than
her wish for sexual union with Forrest and sustains Eva for as much
of her life as we see—even after Bedford's death.

The implicitly sexual quality of the love between parent and child,
which is suggested by Eva's relationship to Bedford and by the repeated image of the incubus, becomes clearer when Forrest mastur-
bates in Eva's absence, taking her phantom body in his head. He
realizes that his union with Eva was itself a substitute for "the oldest
memory of all—with Mother and truly wanted there, at last, no rival"
(46). Since that dream cannot be realized any better with Eva than
alone, Forrest attempts to reconcile himself to solitude. Later, Eva
has a parallel experience of masturbation and recognizes that it will
suffice her; years later, she recommends the same procedure to her
son Rob.

Following the last sexual encounter with Eva, Forrest strips away
their stained bedsheet and instructs himself: "*Alone. Love that. Love
only that. Beyond you is harm, betrayal, theft.*" He recalls a poem
by Catullus concerning a ritual castration and waits for a "balsam
wreath of patience, [sexual] detachment" to settle on his head—but
it does not come, and "he knew it would never" (59). The love
of solitude cannot endure for Forrest, but he must pursue it; so to
reverse love's journey he goes to Panacea Springs, where he pro-

posed to Eva, and finds that appropriately it is being dismantled. That love is not a panacea, that sexual desire is a force that masquerades as love, is suggested when Forrest is told that this spring is nothing special: it will " 'make your pecker work. Like anybody's water' " (61). His informant is Bankey Patterson, an old black who prefigures Robinson Mayfield (of whom Forrest dreams that night) as a self-serving buccaneer; like Robinson, Bankey had abandoned his mother and suffers guilt for that. Even those who are most cynical about love's appeal cannot escape it.

Continuing his ritualized backward journey, Forrest walks home to Bracey. His widowed sister Hatt and black kinsman Grainger are ready to love him and help him patch together a life. Forrest makes a last try at his marriage, when he sends Eva his mother's ring and a wagon for Rob such as Rob Sr. had given to Forrest saying, " '*Forrest and I are bound for bliss!*' " (91). Again, the dream of absolute pleasures, with the failure of a previous generation as background, is resurrected; again, it fails. Forrest goes next to Richmond, to visit the man who welched on his promise of bliss. Rob Sr. is living now in his parental home, having retired there from such exploits as the engendering of Grainger (his grandson) and the abandonment of his wife and children to care for his aged mother until her death. Like Tom Ryden in *A Generous Man*, he is a buccaneer with devastating appeal for women, who blames others (his wife, his son) for having failed to keep him at home. He wants, obviously, both things: freedom and connection. He is "an old sick man still propped round the hole in the midst of his heart which years ago he'd asked even a five-year-old boy to fill" (100). And Forrest, seeing his father alternately as still youthful and attractive, and as a repellent, aged satyr, is ready now to fill it. Again, Rob Sr. rejects him as insufficiently attractive; and this experience seems nearly lethal to Forrest, a repetition of his rejection by Eva. Forrest's mutedly sexual connection to his father, in fact, seems stronger than the oedipal bond to his mother; and this is always the case in *The Surface of Earth*, that a child really loves only one of its parents, and that the chosen parent becomes for the child a paradigmatic lover. Forrest's backward journey is now complete. He has been rejected at the source.

Rob Sr.'s own situation is an elaborate compromise. His current help is Polly, the young woman whose devotion is continuing proof of the buccaneer's appeal. His other companions are the primal dolls he has carved, the parental deities of his final home. Still he complains of loneliness, warning Forrest against it, and at the same time recommending escape tactics which can have no other consequence. Forrest, "at the bottom of his life," awaiting either suicide "or a miracle of grace; some rope lowered to him for rescue, haulage" (114), finds his compromise in the opening supplied by his father's death, reported to him by Polly in the letter which ends Book One. He returns to Richmond and is happier than most, Price suggests, with Polly and his work as a teacher as props to his life.

Book Two: "The Heart in Dreams"

The central section of the novel represents a further definition of the search for absolute pleasures undertaken by Forrest and Eva. Echoes and parallels abound to enforce the sense that history is repeated, or that only one history exists for everyone: the absolute we seek is not obtainable on the earth's surface. This repetition is exemplified by the reappearance of Mayfield forenames—Robinson, Forrest—in successive generations and by the persistently familiar mise-en-scène which the characters inhabit—the same beds, the same windows.

In "The Heart in Dreams" time has advanced seventeen years, to the point where Rob Mayfield, Forrest's and Eva's son, is on the verge of "flight toward his life" (129). His parents have achieved their separate, reasonably happy lives at the expense of their son's absolute pleasure—or so Rob believes. Like his maternal grandmother, Rob is saddled with the knowledge that his birth caused grievous harm. "Prior claims" (150), Eva's need to attend her ailing father, and her insistent, accusatory (and therefore to us, but probably not to Price, unnatural) memory of the difficulty of Rob's birth have led to a certain distance on her part—sufficient for Rob to feel that more than other human beings he deserves and needs "'a lot of goodness'" (260). What we discover, however, is that Rob has had more than his share of goodness from others; the validity of his complaint is questioned on all sides. For Rob, living without the full attention of Eva, the care of Rena, Grainger, and Sylvie is inconsequential—"the same as being alone since he neither wanted nor needed them" (134). He demands too much of Eva, who gives Rob more than he allows, and appreciates too little the love that his attractiveness (inherited from Rob Sr.) wins from others in the

Kendal household. He regards those who have succumbed to his charms as a "dark web of feeders" (129) and wants to escape.

The failure of his oedipal attachment to Eva has led Rob to suppose that consolation resides in "the touch of bodies . . . he'd endowed with the power to save him" (134). He suffers, in fact, from what seems a terminal case of adolescent longing. Eva was the victim of similarly confusing forces. She tells Rob, "*I was paralyzed in woe from twelve years old, when I turned into a woman.*" Because sexuality emerges and is unassuaged at a time when the child's dream of absolute pleasures on the homefront has receded, it exaggerates other lacks (such as both Eva and Rob have felt in relation to their mothers) and appears as a panacea. In fact, as Eva's own experience suggests, the sexual solutions posed at this time may lead to "*deeper trouble*" (280). Rob pursues his fated course, however—demanding on his high school graduation night a sexual initiation from a girl named Min and petulantly discarding her when she refuses to comply. As Rena points out, he "*accept[s] gifts badly*" (182) and the refusal of his demands still worse.

Rob's sense of deprivation with regard to Eva leads him to consider suicide. Even as a child he " 'knew the very gun on [his] grandfather's mantel that would do the trick' " (269). Early in his flight from home, having received Eva's avowal that she does not "demand [his] presence as a means of protection for [her] own future life" (150), Rob presents this to Hatt as grounds that he should follow the example of his suicidal kin. Rob comes closer to suicide during his journey from Goshen to Richmond, when he observes some boys shooting at a turtle in a river. Reflecting that he should " 'maybe end it now—the whole damn relay race . . . with a baton passed by the dead or the useless and no one to take it,' " Rob thinks of offering the spectacle of his suicide as a sign of " 'what they've done' " (191). He refers to his family and to the boys, to all who flagrantly disregard the harm they wreak upon other living creatures. He accepts the turtle as emblematic of his own enforced isolation and vulnerability; like Quentin Compson with the trout in William Faulkner's *The Sound and the Fury*, Rob wants that ancient turtle to survive even if he cannot. The determined antagonism of the young fishermen confirms for Quentin, as the marksmen briefly do for Rob, how untenable is the prospect of continuance. Like Rob's uncle Kennerly, whose father had given him a watch to impress upon him that what mattered was "'just time, killing time'" (297), Quentin receives a watch from his father; and he decides to kill time, to affect his release from a blasted family life, by killing himself. Rob, however, is not so determined to die. His "gifts for joy were natural and large" (134), and hope wins out. Throughout the novel, in fact, Price measures the damage that his characters sustain, and often the language of "killing" is exposed as hyperbolic. His characters can endure considerably more than they suppose.

Rob's despairing journey (like Forrest's) is also a process of recovery through which he begins to be weaned from Eva. His mother, encouraging Rob's self-sufficiency by denying that she needs him, does not endorse his search for a substitute. She tells him that "*the belief that love was the best thing life could give*" is a "*blight*" and that "*a body can be its own solace alone*" (185). She warns him of this because Rob is on the brink of choosing Rachel, the troubled daughter of a hotel-keeper and custodian of a spring in Goshen; and she fears that he is rushing into marriage as a panacea, as she had done. However, when Rob takes his nearly suicidal journey to Richmond and reveals his misery to his long-lost father, as Forrest had done to Rob Sr., Forrest advises him to "'find someone to help you'" (201), as Polly has helped Forrest. The question of how much one can expect from marriage becomes pronounced at this point. Forrest's life with Polly seems to Rob "a first-rate imitation of contentment" (204). Rob's is "The Heart in Dreams," however: he thinks his portion should include not only a perfect marriage, "*happiness and finally rest*," but the obvious impossibility of "*two parents . . . in their own large house which he and his older brother and sister visit on Sundays*" (195). He wants to provide a script not only for the future, but for the past.

The less idyllic relationship of Forrest and Polly has the advantage of being real. But that Price offers this as the book's only lasting and desirable approximation of marriage suggests his belief that the Bible is not far wrong in portraying (as Rob Sr. had complained) "'Not one happy pair, not one that lasts long enough to watch and learn *how* from'" (104). Forrest's union with Polly is a peculiar one: they make love only ten times a year, presumably because greater intimacy would defeat their enterprise. Women, Forrest believes, are capable of protracted attention in love, while men are not. The formula for success seems a kind of compromise between marriage and solitude, such as Polly permits. She cheerfully serves Forrest and accepts his decision not to marry her, but she is not entirely secure; their success is both revered and restricted by the novelist, to convey what he perceives as the almost insurmountable difficulty of a paired existence.

Rob now returns to Goshen and asks Rachel to " 'live out a life' " (221) with him. Inauspiciously, however, it seems that he has chosen without due consideration of his desire for this particular girl. Polly had suggested he " 'pick the strong one' " (214), but Rachel's illness and her intense need of Rob may cause us to question the wisdom of his choice. Rob congratulates himself on the freedom of his decision, but later writes to Eva that she is *"back of this"* and that Rachel *"is in certain ways a likeness of"* (233) his mother. It seems, therefore, that Rob has not succeeded in following the advice offered by both his parents—to sever his oedipal bond with Eva. Forrest had expressed this with a quotation from the *Aeneid*, in which the mother goddess advises her son to *"proceed and walk with the road"* (223), to pursue a fate separate from her. Despite these elements of foreboding, there is sufficient ambiguity in the portrait of Rachel to suggest that Rob's desperate action may result in success. Rachel declares she is *"nothing if not lasting"* (178) and Rob describes her as *"a hard little scrapper"* (180). Rachel's own admission that Rob is " *'built for harm'* " (243) is courageously modified by her assertion that *"ruin"* may come as easily through *"the beefsteak we ate for supper"* (244); she is determined to be happy and not to collapse in the face of risk.

The centerpiece of the novel, the dinner on the eve of the wedding, draws together nearly all factions concerned in the union. The occasion provides an opportunity for revelation and prophecy, and there is a suggestion of divine blessing as Grainger passes out brandy glasses "as carefully as if he had transmuted water itself for these guests." The most significant oratory comes from Forrest, who presents this marriage as something that nobody " 'had any right to plan for, dream for, expect.' " He calls it a victory for all concerned, and a triumph over the persistent psychological traits of the Mayfields, who are inveterate leavers and do not like pain. But the attractiveness of bride and groom, he argues, is " 'no guarantee that life [will] prove yielding,' " so that to the catalog of failures which he offers as backdrop he adds the clear warning that their victory may not last. Still, Forrest intends to be optimistic; he asserts that things that make us " 'yearn to last' " are " '*sent,* not accidents of time' " (248), and Grainger echoes this in his claim that grace and happiness will come

" 'if you be patient.' " Again the optimism is undercut, as Grainger's
wife Gracie remarks " 'Nothing finished' " (250)—grace cannot be
relied upon, and old troubles are still potent.

In a series of confrontations following the dinner, the risks and
chances of Rob's marriage continue to be assessed. From Rena, he
learns that " 'a single journey is a dry rag to suck' " (252); and
Rena, although her solitary life has had its consolations (mainly her
intense, inadequately requited love of Rob), should know. To Della,
the black girl who has catered to Rob's sexual needs, he affirms that
he will keep his promise to Rachel because " 'she's the person who
has asked' " (264); the irony, of course, is that numerous others have
asked for Rob's life. Rob doubts "his own strength of purpose, the
durability of present intentions" (267); he senses that anything
"might rupture the paper walls he's propped round the cube of space
at the core of his chest, walls he'd shown to Rachel as permanent
ramparts" (253). Finally he realizes that in the absence of love for
Rachel he has "chosen something lonelier than solitude," a "quick
resort to remedies as harsh as any his mother had seized as a girl."
His only solace is that "time would teach him to take her" (272).

Time is not granted, however, in sufficient quantity. Rachel dies
in giving birth to Hutch, not long after Rob has learned to love
her—the familiar promise to God is unavailing, and the prelude to
Rachel's death is a bout of drinking inspired by Rob's guilt over a
single instance of buccaneer-like infidelity with his old girl friend
Min. (All of this is recounted in Book Three.) The death fulfills
an old fear of Rachel's which is also a wish. Like Rob, Rachel has
a rapacious need for love, "*some strange starvation in the core of
the heart*" (244). Her father's love was insufficient because it was
directed to " 'the likeness of his mother' " (269) which he saw in
Rachel; and before Rob's arrival at Goshen, she had induced a psycho-
somatic pregnancy as her bid for life. At the same time, she was
tempted by death. Then Rob appeared, and Rachel was again determined to live. Later, however, characters such as her friend Alice
confirm that Rachel did not believe (despite her protestations to
Rob) that she would last. She demands from Rob the right to let
herself "*truly risk what* [she] *played at before—simple creation*"
(284). Her ultimate demand is the right to adhere to her prophetic,
almost mystical vision. Her certainty, her "patience to plead . . . gifts
from life" (312) whether harmful or pleasant, stems finally from her
conviction that the "*place in glory*" (187) for which she waits can

be found in the creation of a child, if life permits, or in death. Thus Rachel in her intensity, in her visionary and paradoxical attractions to both life and death, comes close to revealing that the heart's dreams will be permanently satisfied only when the soul returns to God.

Book Three: "Partial Amends"

The third Mayfield odyssey belongs to Hutch, who at fourteen sets out from the Kendal home earlier than had either Eva or Rob. He too suffers guilt in relation to his mother and pain from the inadequacy of parental attention. Surrounded by people who love him, Hutch is waiting for Rob to return to Fontaine and claim him. He does not count on sexuality as an answer to his woes, however; and he is destined to be an artist, so that valuable work may help him to resolve the solitude vs. contingency question in a reasonably satisfying manner. His father's life journey is proceeding badly. Rachel is sorely missed and Forrest newly dead; Rob is drinking heavily and has lost his teaching post in Raleigh. Rob's expectations have been lowered to the point where he considers a self-sacrificial marriage to Min, to thank her for years of sexual help. Pressured by Min to make a decision, Rob sets out on a journey which will test other options, other wrongs he might prefer to right. It is a search for absolution, an attempt to " 'take the people who are present, and ignore the poor dead' " (327). The immediate impetus is his promise of a trip to Hutch, "*the one human* [he has] *vowed God to live for*" (330).

On the way to Fontaine Rob gives a lift to Bo Parker and tells him the story of Rachel's death. Rob's tale is presented to the black man as an instance of the incongruity between God's benevolence and human suffering. Recalling Forrest, who taught his classes that "*God wants us to understand life as a comedy*" (286), Bo sees his own coming death and Rachel's as part of God's plan and Rob's suffering as His way of " 'calling you to Him' " (339). Further, he denies Rob's guilt: " 'Nobody blame a poor man for what Jesus do' " (334). Following this encounter, Rob senses that "a vein had been lanced." Grief surfaces "from the deepest sink of his belly" with apparently lethal force; he survives, recalls and rejects the possibility of suicide, and has been more renewed than he knows by these "throes of expulsion" (340). He has begun, in fact, to forgive himself for Rachel's death and is ready for the next phase of his life to begin.

In Fontaine Rob stops first at Sylvie's house—receiving food and blame and assurance that the modified single life is possible: " 'Live in what you got' " (345). At the Kendal home he finds Hutch asleep and lies on him in the familiar position of incubus. But Rob still wants more than Hutch. The combination he seeks is an opportunity to pay some of his debts, company which includes sexual consolation, a home, and a decent job. He makes a first try at this in a visit to Thorne Bradley; the combination is to include Hutch and Min and a teaching job in Fontaine. Like Rena, from whom Rob learns that " 'even strong old boats have been known to plummet on calm summer days' " (373), and like Min, who affirms that men can " 'sink in broad day with the waters calm beneath them' " (327), Thorne acknowledges that Rob might easily become " 'one more drowned life' " (356). He offers him the job, but the opportunity is no guarantee of success: Rob can still plummet if he chooses to indulge in self-pity. What can help, as both Kennerly and Rena make clear to Rob, are realistic expectations and patience. Kennerly's advice is to " 'Come to life' " (378). Rob can live anywhere, but must not expect " 'perfect peace . . . a happy life. You can dream that forever.' " Life, Kennerly says, is " 'just a long wait' " (379) for the peace that is available only in death. And Rena offers scriptural support of that view.

Rob leaves for Virginia Beach with Hutch, who dreams of a life in which they " 'could watch each other, really watch all day' " (402). Rob explains his neglect of Hutch by asserting his "taste for human touch' " (395), his desire for sex—and goes with Hutch to a strip show, which is incomprehensible to the boy. Hutch is an avid masturbator and cannot think why another person should be required for erotic gratification. In fact, the strip show fails to justify Rob's hunger for a woman's body; it implies frustration rather than a salutary pursuit. Hutch resents Min because she reveals this need in Rob, which he cannot satisfy and thinks should not exist. Asserting his own need, Hutch assumes the position of incubus on his father's body—easing them both, though "nothing was cured" (403).

They proceed to Richmond, where an embittered Polly criticizes the choice made by Pocahontas to leave her own people because of love. The tale of the Indian girl is a favorite of Grainger's and more recently of Hutch; its appeal resides in the affirmation of a romantic vision, the possibility of removal from a life that is judged inferior to some distant, unworkable ideal. Gracie calls it one of " 'them dream books' " (435), citing it as a cause of Grainger's racial discontentment. Polly's anger arises from her sense of abandonment, the harsh discovery that Forrest has made no provision for her. Having risked her heart in dreams that seemed modest enough, Polly now regrets the forfeit of her " 'own place that [her] mother died to give [her]' " (405). Reflecting on Polly's need and on the attractions of Forrest's life under her care, Rob considers whether he and Hutch should move in with Polly. He rejects this, however, because Polly and Hutch are " 'too old, too young, misshaped to his [sexual] purpose' " (428). "Men and women,' " he tells Hutch, " 'are as separate as rabbits and cats' " (422); women hide their loneliness in families, but men in a "blind clamor" (417) persist in the search for sexual consolation. And Rob is still not ready to dispense with that brand of help.

Rob's "blind clamor," however, is abusive and parasitic, depositing in Rob with each indulgence the heavy burden of guilt. In a dream Rob discovers Della in a field in wartime France. She assures him that she is protected, secure with " 'My ring you give me.' " The ring, Rob feels, "had some right to be there," but he silently confesses to Della " 'I gave you nothing; you'll die before night' " (413). Even less than Polly or Min has Della been recompensed for her loving gifts; the Mayfield men take, but give too little. Gracie asserts that some women want (and certainly they tolerate) abuse, but the issue with Min is that Rob must avoid further abuse. She declines any postponement of Rob's decision to choose her honorably as his wife; Hutch, at the same time, declines any arrangement that includes Min. And Rob cannot reconcile the two, so he collapses into drunkenness. Hutch finds Rob naked on the floor and pleading for rest, which Hutch understands as a signal for his departure. Covering the shame of his father's nakedness (which recalls that of the biblical Noah), Hutch sets out for Goshen.

He makes what for the Mayfield questers seems an obligatory stop in Bracey. Like Rob, Hutch is briefly tempted by Hatt's offer of refuge; because she confuses him with Forrest, Hutch fantasizes that a quiet life presided over by her delusion would effectively cancel the past, undo the damage of several generations. But he moves on to Goshen, to find that Raven Hutchins is dead and has left the hotel to Della. Like Bankey at Panacea Springs, Della distrusts this casual gift from white hands, and she gives the hotel to Hutch, as Grainger later will give him the Mayfield family ring. She also absolves Hutch of blame for his mother's death, telling him that " 'Rachel died doing all Rachel ever tried to do' " (454). Hutch decides that he has been fitted to a "full set of harness to which any number of people held reins, some of them stone-dead," and he chooses "to wear it" (461). This commitment moves him through a baptismal rite at the spring and on to "the source of dreams" (462), a shrine to Rachel. There he meets Alice, his mother's closest friend, a further link to the past and a beacon for his future.

Alice is an artist. As a child she had prayed for a room " 'with a one-way lock and a window that would see *out* but not show [her]' " (468–69). She believed that from there she could " 'spy on the world,' " understand and draw its beauty, and then come forth to reap love for her work. But with adolescence she decided that " 'the world came *paired*,' " and her previous isolation seemed " '*blessed*' " (469) in comparison with the misery of seeking a lover. She acknowledges to Hutch the power of wanting to " 'magnetize some perfectly plain human face and rush helpless to it' " (470), but asserts that her greatest desire (and the world's) is to be still. Hutch's version of this is " 'to be still next to someone you want in a place where there's no extra people in sight,' " but Alice corrects him: " 'Just the *still* part, I think. Other people come later and are mostly mistakes' " (468). She also analyzes the attempt màde by Rob and Rachel; echoing Kennerly, she argues that their mistake was to believe they could have " 'their wishes fulfilled,' " because " 'wishes are dreams . . . [not] orders which the world will obey' " (467). Her advice implies that Hutch, though he will continue as Alice does to yearn for love, may be reconciled to solitude.

Work and intermittent company will make the difference. Hutch senses this as he and Alice sketch the landscape from their separate ledges. He realizes that his drawing is "not what he'd seen or was seeing now" (471). But Hutch is patient, content to accept his approximations and "wait till the secret of leaves . . . came into his power" (472). Taken "from what the earth offered of its visible skin," his effort has been "to watch; then grope for its heart" (471), a return to the world of the world's gifts. Patience and close scrutiny are essential, for the mystery that the world conceals may be "good news" or "news of hatred"; any "leaf," (472) or object of study such as Rob's face, may be demonic or benevolent—and the artist's job is to see the truth. Although the world in Price's view is finally comic,

Hutch (like Price himself) will not shrink from the harsh appearances which are cast up for his steady gaze.

Rob arrives that evening in search of Hutch. He first encounters Della, from whom he begs a familiar form of help; but his attitude to Della is more appreciative than usual, an attempt at partial amends. He feels that he has always "meant only good to the world and himself and would live to achieve it as the trees do leaves" (478). Min's final refusal is now in hand, and Rob imagines a possible life for himself in Goshen. One barrier to that is his son's mistrust. Hutch knows that parents have "infinite power to turn in an instant into monsters" (479); he has learned that at Richmond and survived the sight. But he still fears Rob's aberrations and is reluctant even to speak of Alice, since Rob "might like her too much" (481). Hutch values the relationship that he is cultivating with Alice and does not want it damaged for either of them by Rob's attractive, insistent, and unreliable presence. Alice also values Hutch, in whom she sees the vestiges of her love for Rachel (a parallel to Thorne's love for Forrest); she sees in his eyes "the passion for absolute pleasure, the soul's reward" (473), which through art and friendship may reach a safe, joyful fruition.

In a bid for the boy's faith, Rob tells the story of his wedding night. He says that had he been allowed the time to study " 'what Rachel's face meant' " after lovemaking, the angels would have found " 'no mortal fault' " (484) in him. But an angel of Judgment (the harbinger of Rachel's early death) came too soon in Rob's dream, as a porter came too soon in their hotel. By the time Rob was ready to look again at Rachel's transfigured face, she had gone to God. The parallel to Hutch's study of the leaves is clear; and Price offers this story as his strongest proof that love between man and woman can be "an entrance" (472) to the world's core. Rob uses it to suggest a new willingness to possess his heart in patience: " 'People get what they need if they stand still and watch till the earth sends it up ... What they need, not want' " (484).

Hutch invites his father to join him in " 'the master bed' " where Rob again reflects that this child's body was "not sufficient to have held him true" to the promise made at Rachel's death. But he is aware of their "juncture" or "natural bond" (486) and recalls a comparable "quick space of knowledge, prophetic and true"—the sight of Eva, loving him. He realizes that out of his parents' attempt at

absolute pleasure had come "a son made from their lives but stronger—
to perfect their purpose and transmit it" (487). Their dreams of
marriage failed, but by an alternate path he had been "steered and
saved." Through the devotion of "the single and barren" Rob has survived; he "honored their strength now and prayed for them." This
speech of praise in honor of the novel's solitaries is a counterbalance
to the scene of Rachel's transfiguration. And Rob, to transmit the
favor he has received, now reaffirms his promise to Hutch, to "stay
in place wherever they landed and watch Hutch closely till Hutch
said *Stop*" (488). He will help and not intrude and will control
his own "blind clamor."

In the final scene of the novel Grainger arrives with news of Bo's
death and Sylvie's grief—to which Rob reacts with laughter. The
humor he feels comes from Bo's own vision of a comic existence, in
which grief serves no purpose. As a confirmation of his vision, of
God's design amidst the apparent chaos of "something [which] crashed
in the kitchen" (491), the Mayfield ring fashioned generations earlier
finds a perfect fit on Hutch's left hand.

Imagery

The persistence of the author's special view of human relationships is attested to by his use of images and diction that are familiar
from earlier works. Hatt's regret, for example, that she gave Forrest
inadequate attention because of her " 'own life sucking hard at [her]' "
(19) recalls the sucking images, the draining of resources, in *A Long
and Happy Life*. The incubus image recalls the vampires of *Love and
Work* and *Permanent Errors*. Names and faces, signposts of individuality and genetic fate, continue to be important. Forrest, for example, told that he is "his father's mirror," searches his face and finds
that it is "open as a plate" (47); and Hutch, abandoning his hope
of a life with Rob, studies his face to draw his own portrait, a
"memorial of what he was leaving for this new life" (446). Polly,
like Rosacoke, insists on being called by her name; and characters are
regularly assessed in terms of how much Kendal or Watson or Mayfield they have in their blood. The language of love as food and of
exchange, of gifts and thanks and reward and debt and promise,
also contributes to the steady maintenance in *The Surface of Earth*
of the author's familiar vision.

The most important image patterns in the novel, however, are those that surround a dialogue between the earth's surface and its core. Briefly, this is the relationship between frenetic activity on the surface of the globe and underlying generative forces, the wellspring, it seems, of strife and happiness. Much of the book's action, for example, is played out against a distant backdrop of two world wars. This allows a perspective by which to measure the exaggerated suffering of characters like Rob, but it also expands the geographical microcosm through which they move into a vision of the globe's surface as inimical to peace. Rob's desire for solace and at times surcease is presented in a dream where, suffering from tuberculosis, he " 'must walk on up in the mountains to the springs' " (319). His journey is punctuated by sounds of battle, but near death he finds his cure in Rachel, the springs of love. Clearly, the adversity of Rob's life is imaged by war; similarly, Hutch, suffering from the absence of both parents, dreams "of children . . . seated far apart in a bare Norman field, consumed by real flames—no man in sight or hearing, no woman" (488).

These creatures who ply the earth's surface are not devoid of hope. Regularly, they leave what are perceived as intolerable situations in search of someone or some place where " 'life will happen' " (50). The compulsion simply for movement is illustrated, following Eva's rejection of him, by Forrest's desire for "physical motion—to be out of this place and into another" (73). Roads, of course, are natural vehicles for this impulse, and significantly Rob's job in Goshen is to build a road. The use of such work is mainly that it will " 'wear [him] out till something harder comes' " (199), a sentiment echoed by Gracie who is hunting *"what will use* [her] *up, what will burn* [her] *down"* (314). Roads do not "guarantee your destination" and can land the traveler "in oblivion or punishment" (330). " 'To blow up rocks' " (199) in roadbuilding, as Rob does, may be simply to expend one's energy on the surface of the earth; ultimately, as that image suggests, the real direction of the search is not horizontal but vertical. Images of mining or digging or sinking move an individual closer to "the core of force" (78), to *"whatever's in the heart of the ground"* (163).

Sexual activity is perhaps the central activity through which such vertical movement is attempted. When Forrest makes love to Eva he senses in her that "every entrance was free; every channel conductive to the center of joy" (25), and later he imagines himself above Eva, "her face as open as a mine at work" (46). Grainger and Gracie,

we are told, "dug and worked in one another" (258). Sex offers
momentary liberation, an interval of peace more satisfying than the
horizontal search. Della, for instance, after orgasm is "a distant county
of a country at peace" (216). Sexual pleasure attracts, pulls one's
attention *like great magnets in the earth*" (12), but as a "threat
to kill" (46) sex is linked with death, "the downward haul of the
earth" (195). The variety of magnetic forces—sex, death, Hutch's
wish to be a magnet for Rob, the Kendal household—suggests that
the world is rife with unreliable approximations of a deeper, more
satisfying peace. The peace of death through suicide is not endorsed
in the novel, and sex is ultimately for Rob only a nerve that is
" 'numbed . . . awhile' " (489). The search for company, the need
to " 'magnetize one perfectly plain human face' " (470), is often
deceptive and unrewarding. The overall intention behind the proliferation of magnetic imagery, however, is to reveal the desire for "a
piece of the one precious heart of things, the satisfied whole toward
which parts yearned" (130).

The existence of this core is manifested on the earth's surface in
the form of mineral springs and to some extent in trees, their foliage
sustained by sap deep within the trunk. Such manifestations are vulnerable, however; springs can become foul and clogged, and trees can
suffer blight. Grainger erects a shed with a cedar roof over the
springs in Goshen, and to protect themselves people construct spaces
in their heads, in houses, or as Polly does in the " 'cupboard' " (256)
of someone else's life. Eva lives in "the small dry room in the front
of her skull," a room which like Alice's dream room has "one door
[that] opened outward only" (238). Forrest builds around himself
a "frail but roofing shed . . . a roof made of pride in his gift for
solitude" (73), which soon collapses; Bedford, similarly, predicts that
Eva will " 'cave in like a shed' " (138) at his death. The imagery of
private spaces is not restricted to buildings on land, for the earth's
surface also contains oceans. Forrest, for example, sees Hatt's house
as a "ship with skeleton crew" (22), and Rob finds safety in Della's
room, "a sealed ship plowing the night" (259). All such refuge is
ultimately vulnerable, however. The image of Forrest's frail shed
is echoed in that of the turtle besieged by thoughtless boys and by
numerous images of melons. Min's belly, like Rob's, is called an
" 'abandoned melon' " (235), and Rob leaves a melon (a shell with
a heart) for Gracie, which she refuses because it " 'give me dreams
this late' " (437).

The rooms, both marine and terrestrial, and particularly the melons are essentially a repetition of the larger image of the earth and its core. The dichotomy of an inner and outer world is sustained, too, by the frequent use of images of boils and fistulas, manifestations of deeper forces at work altering the surface. Man in his separate micro-cosm is like the "giant in a cave who was dreaming the world" (472), and characters often project onto the ceilings of their separate cham-bers wishes which seem unattainable. The most central image of such hopeful dreaming is Rob's attempt "to write with his mind on the patient plaster surface" (195) an ideal past and future. Dreams of a perfect life collapse with the death of Rachel, however, and their destruction is marked by another ceiling image. He writes Polly that he lost his teaching job because he "*cried one day in the midst of explaining how you calculate the quantity of plaster needed to cover the ceiling of a hotel ballroom*" (238).

Dreams, then, are not guarantees of happiness. The benevolent giant at the heart of the earth might prove to be "the jeering mask of a demon" (472), and spring water may act as "poison or balm" (229). Trees which symbolize human growth—Rob's "thickening trunk" (40)—may live to produce leaves or may wither, a danger to others. Casualties are inevitable in a world suffering from "gen-eral famine," though "saving kernel[s]" (160) such as Grainger do exist. Although it appears impossible that "trees . . . would leaf again; that they would not refuse and stand in their skeletons" (29), Price asserts that "'most people die smiling or are happy till the last . . . their needs get filled'" (366). Rob's arrival at such an end is ulti-mately not contingent upon his efforts to achieve it, but rather upon the caprice of a "spirit . . . from the patient earth, bearing freight that the caller had not foreseen" (483). In a world which "*is funny since* [God] *knows the outcome*" (286), the best one can do to wrest happiness from life is to find "a place to stand in till the world showed its core, its secret news, its reward to his patient watch on its skin" (486).

The Dreams

There are at least twenty dreams in *The Surface of Earth*, and as Della says, they are "'always true'" (263). The most profound of these is granted to Eva: it is a dream of peace, where Eva finds herself "'in the school . . . the only one'" (97), with people who know what

they are there to learn, though she does not. These angelic scholars
have a gift that is denied to Price's daytime people; their attention,
we surmise, is focused upon God. In nearly all the other dreams
people are concerned with the loss and gain of one another. Often
they dream of recovering dead parents and of losing them again, of
abandonment, of troubled journeys, of forsaken children, and of
death. The background for many of these dreams is war, the ultimate killer. But the truest of all true dreams is Eva's, the dream of
peace which resides on the other side of all the dreams of death and
drowning and dissolves their pain. Dreams come from something
larger than a single consciousness. Rob's dream of Rachel is completed by Min, for instance. Sylvie's dream of a child in need of
rescue (presumably Hutch) is intended as a blessing for Grainger
and connects with Rachel's two dreams of drowning. Dreams establish secret arches for the novelist, as when Rob dreams of Hatt cleaning out a stable; this establishes her likeness to Rena, another un-
thanked worker, who in a photograph is shown at a stable, similarly
yearning for a son. The dreams illustrate not only an individual
character's deepest fears and hopes, but also the author's sense of a
common life journey for all his people. They all enter dreams through
water, and all are searching for the earth's perfect core.

The Blacks

Characteristic of all odysseys are those individuals who contribute
to the success of the quester's search. Often numinous in nature or
possessing clairvoyant abilities, they bear messages, identify hidden
danger, and provide sustenance in various forms. In *The Surface of
Earth* these services are supplied by blacks who either work as servants in white households or roam the countryside, still requiring the
opportunity to serve. Their realistic portrayal is limited by Price's
emphasis upon a symbolic function. They fulfill a dual purpose, at
times providing the archetypal services of a guiding angel, and at
other times reflecting in their own lives the dilemmas that confront
the whites. Such dilemmas, the search for rest or love or lost parents,
seem to the whites considerably more interesting when they occur in
their own lives, and the irony of this self-absorption is strongly
pointed by Price, in honor of the blacks.

Grainger, for example, is described by Forrest as "*Hermes . . . elo-
quent herald, conductor of souls*" (48) when he brings Eva's letter;

but his own parallel relations with Gracie, his attempts through her and also through his Mayfield kin "to find that childhood of perfect assurance" (258), are not sufficiently acknowledged. The spiritual dimension of blacks is enforced by numerous classical and biblical links. Veenie's room "seemed also a relic of the Flood" (78); and her aged hands (she is a survivor of the Civil War) give her an antediluvian, almost inhuman appearance—"brown prehensile tentacles of sea-life, blind but infallible" (79). Her benevolence is established, however, when Forrest recalls that "Veenie had simply materialized throughout his youth when his mother needed help" (76). Her descendant Grainger, a mixture of human and divine (or white and black) blood, recalls Christ at Rob's wedding, changing water to wine, and has convinced Hutch that blacks are " 'like angels here to guard us' " (398). Like Bankey, the caretaker at Panacea Springs—or "Elysium" (62)—who employs his "organ of knowledge" to sense "safety, pleasure, rest" (68), Grainger is equipped with a "vane for detecting the weather of any moment" (122).

Female blacks are no less endowed. Della reveals and explains the world of the subconscious through her life's companion, *The Book of Dreams*, and Sylvie (like Grainger) is a messenger in tune with the content of what she brings. Even Gracie, whose attitude is generally defiant, at a revivalist meeting falls into a state of rapture and proclaims that she has been " 'Near to Heaven' " (170). An attribute common to all these characters, male or female, and one that strengthens the overall image of the black as an intermediary between the earth's surface and its hidden sustaining heart, is the ability (of Bo Parker, for instance) to sense events before their occurrence. All arrivals seem expected, all news past knowledge.

Although the racism of the white characters is arrogant and repugnant, its force is modified by some degree of genuine affection for the blacks, and by the archetypal configuration that Price finds in the relationship of the quester and his assistant. Like the white solitaries in the novel, blacks are inadequately thanked. Polly, for instance, recognizes the analogy between her own and Grainger's service of the Mayfields; she is offended by this, aware that she also is dependent upon the goodwill of men who have refused to acknowledge her officially. And she takes it out on Grainger, refusing to wash his underwear since she is not " 'the brown one' " (410). Still, the insult to Polly or to the blacks is emphasized less than the good that their devotion accomplishes. The thanks that blacks often demand for services either sexual or domestic—their "frugal diet" (144)—serve to assert the moral imperative which lies close to the heart of the novel: the dignity which comes from helping others, which Rob also learns. For the impoverished and abused black angel, money is necessary and often accepted, but as Sylvie declares " 'Money . . . don't buy me' " (133). Although blacks have little power to enforce payment, their recurrent refusal of money in lieu of adequate appreciation suggests that to some extent at least the Christian ideal of service is its own reward. Gratitude is more important for the spiritual welfare of its donor than for its recipient.

In Christian theology the angelic administration is intended to service not its own needs but those of God's creation. Thus Bankey Patterson is ultimately correct when in offering to go with Forrest he asserts " 'I *helping* myself' " (71), for whatever the realistic advantages of such a course might be for Bankey, he is also fulfilling his angelic obligations. Grainger, we are told, is " 'waiting on . . . the Mayfields' " (196) for recognition, and he never gets that; but Grainger can transcend personal bitterness to rejoice in waiting on them in another sense. Sylvie's prophetic dream of Hutch promises him a "blessing" (316), a chance to exercise his " 'wings' " (491) and to find a worthy bearer for his ring of devotion.

The Biblical Dimension

Price has said that the biblical translations that appeared as *A Palpable God* were undertaken in part as "preparations for a novel," *The Surface of Earth*. They were "attempts at the purification of [his] own language";[5] and indeed the style of this novel is more strikingly biblical than is usually the case with Price's work. He said also that two of the stories he had chosen to translate bore closely on the intended novel: the rescue of Isaac and the sacrifice of Jephthah's daughter. Both stories concern harsh covenants with God—in the former God relents, and in the latter He does not. And that is essentially the vision of Price's novel: rescue from woe may come in this life, but it cannot be relied upon. The promise that Price's own father made to God, and that Rob makes in the novel, suggests the relevance of the Abraham and Isaac story. The novel is in part a father-and-son love story, played out against a background (only dimly perceived by the characters) of man's ultimately more significant and parallel relationship to God. Jephthah's daughter is an analogue for Rachel, the well-loved daughter who knows that she must die and mourns her virginity in a mountain place. Neither story, of course, is closely followed.

Other biblical stories are alluded to briefly in the novel—the story of Noah's ark and his nakedness, for instance. More significant, however, than such allusions or than occasional, direct quotations from the Bible is the natural recurrence of biblical themes within Price's own narrative imagination. We may well recall, for instance, the passage in Exodus (34:7) which speaks of the sins of the fathers being visited upon the sons unto the third and fourth generations, but we sense that Price's working out of that pattern in his narrative is intrinsic—more fundamental, that is, than any allusive intent. Suffering, sacrifice, retribution, love, covenants, genealogy, the search for the father or home, and the yearning for rest—all of these biblical themes and more work naturally in *The Surface of Earth*.

Although the characters refer easily to the Christian God and Judgment, they do not sufficiently examine their lives in that context or receive the consolation that Price believes is waiting for them. They exist too much on the surface of earth and dwell upon their sufferings. A stronger faith would help them, as Price suggests with Rob's desire for a "life of Jesus telling more than the Gospels" (203) and Hutch's dream of "a book explaining what was not told of Jesus in the King James Bible" (460). They want more evidence. But their restlessness and doubt, Price suggests through his epigraph from St. Augustine, may be endemic to the human condition:

> But You, the Good which needs no good,
> rest always, being Yourself Your rest.
> What man can teach another man that?
> What angel an angel?
> What angel a man?

Black angels cannot teach the whites where rest is to be found, or learn it for themselves. Still, Price assures us in *The Surface of Earth* that rest will come, that " 'the sufferings of this present time are not worthy to be compared with the glory which shall be revealed in us' " (371).[6] In the end of this divine comedy, the gold ring will also fit our hands.

Chapter Eight

The Source of Light

Introduction and Plot Summary

Predictably, reviewers have asked whether *The Source of Light* relies too far on *The Surface of Earth* as its own source of light. Each book does certainly gain in interest from the connection, but it is a strength of the later book (with lesser, attendant disadvantages) that Price resists extensive recapitulation of history given in *The Surface of Earth*. The sequel is narrower in scope, involving some panoramic review as Hutch says his elaborate farewells and Rob prepares for death, but its focus is sufficiently upon Hutch and the here and now that we may feel with the protagonist a sense of release as well as of responsibility to the past. Rob also feels a sense of release, and the novel as a whole seems less claustrophobic, less dark than its predecessor. Genetic determinism is still powerfully at work; imagery, dreams, and letters testify still to a vision of life as repetition, a world of echoes. Yet Hutch and Rob both seem happy about their fates. Indeed, in this book the giant at the center of the earth seems more likely to be smiling at his creatures.

Blacks are still serving and delivering messages in dark angelic fashion. Grainger, for instance, in collaboration with Sylvie, informs Hutch of his father's coming death; later he lets Hutch know that an abortion plan is underway. Integration is now an issue for many of the characters, but the blend of anger and love between the races, understanding and the lack of it, continues as before. The ring that closed the circle of *Surface* has the same function here, journeying from Ann to Polly. And humor, a necessary leavening agent in *The Surface of Earth*, is in *The Source of Light* more evident, more natural, and more satisfying.

The action of the novel takes Hutch, who is now twenty-five, from May, 1955 through March, 1956. It is divided into three sections of decreasing size to reflect his progress toward a goal, a narrowing of choices. In "The Principle of Perturbations" Hutch leaves home, travels in England before settling down to his studies at Oxford, and reflects upon the attractions of assorted male and female lovers, as well as upon Rob and solitude and work. Rob in the meantime is dying of lung cancer, news which is concealed from Hutch. "The Rotation of Venus" describes first Hutch's idyll in Rome with Ann, which inclines him toward marriage and in fact involves the conception of a child; it then veers away, toward Rob—whose imminent death causes Hutch to return home. Rob dies, and Hutch again departs for Oxford. In "The Center of Gravity" Ann has an abortion; abandoned in Rome, she had indulged in a single act of infidelity and so does not know that the child belongs to Hutch. The novel ends with Hutch looking forward to his work as a poet and intermittent, variable company.

Hutch's Plan

The protagonist's choices will be important not only for Hutch, but also for those who regard him as *"the Family Hope."*[1] That term suggests both the seriousness of his endeavor and the danger of an inflated sense of self-importance of which Hutch is humorously, fortunately aware. What is not entirely clear in the novel is whether Price thinks that such examples of self-irony (together with demonstrations of self-control such as are found in Hutch's graceful, carefully nonjudgmental behavior to Ann following the abortion) should preclude our further criticism of his hero. There is a considerable distance between Hutch and characters such as Thomas Eborn and Charles Tamplin whose satirical portraits also have drawn upon the author's crucial life experience: the death of his parents, his profession, travels, and so on. But while Hutch is a vastly more attractive person than either Eborn or Tamplin, he is still a romantic egoist. Self-obsessed, he is also self-righteous—witness, for instance, his claim that *"So far as I understand the Ten Commandments, I've never broken one"* (148). It is difficult to know whether Price finds that assertion safe; his immediate purpose is to establish Hutch's lack of guilt for his sexual conduct, and he may believe that Hutch's adjoining, partial confession to the deadly sin of pride makes the larger claim invulnerable to our attack—our laughter or distaste.

Much of the novel is concerned with the fine tunings and drastic shifts of key that Hutch contemplates for his life plan. He begins with a need for distance from familial "nets" and "webs," a need which Rob accommodates by keeping his disease a secret. Hutch knows then and more clearly by the end of the novel that distance of various kinds will provide him with a perspective from which to observe and (if his gift serves) to memorialize his family history. Rob says that the family *"would be grateful if anyone looked back on us (not down) and saw that we'd made anything like a diagram in these fifty years"*—since the Kendal and Mayfield genes commingled, that is. He suggests that *"all of us may have earned a kind of peace in you, earned it for you."* He thinks Hutch is destined to make that diagram, not only by his intelligence, but because somehow he has *"escaped having whatever worm gnawed us"*—a worm that wanted happiness, *"from other humans, here and now"* (56). Still Hutch is not sure. Perhaps love, a "well-paired life" which he has "never doubted" is the "central aim" of most human existence, is the means by which he can redeem his family's past. Sometimes he believes that both love and work are possible to him. But Hutch suspects that he has been *"designated* by whatever hand of God, Fate, The Past to stand on the edge alone and stare inward steadily." That is a more attractive explanation for his probable exclusion from that "central aim" than the possibility that he is "lame or scared" (39) of love.

Hutch looks forward to proving himself as a solitary artist—"a born outrider capable of calling in useful reports or a driven scout on solitary missions of value to groups huddled nearer the fire" (40). But he is not sure that he is capable of living alone; he wants also to be a "warmer" and to be warmed himself. If he does opt for love (beyond the "fun" of masturbation endorsed by all his family), there are further complications: who the lover is to be, which sex, and whether the same person would consistently (and not overbearingly) suffice. In the end, Hutch seems reconciled to "a solitary journey with skirmishes of company" (292); his "happiness" will not be dependent upon *"other humans, here and now."*

There is also the question of Hutch's ability to perform the task at hand. As in the leaf-drawing scene from *Surface*, patience seems the first requirement: *"all I know how to give is what I seem better at than anything else—the patience to watch things (people mainly) and copy their motions. I hope that will somehow prove a means of love, of finding the place where each thing is still and will no longer leave"* (317). The faculty of attention, which is necessary if flux is to be seen through and permanence or rest achieved, is here transferred from the realm of human love (where it is doomed to failure) to the parallel realm of art—in which success is possible, in which the beloved is honored by accuracy of vision and the artist-lover cannot be betrayed. Beauty will be served by watching: "No touch, no friction, no wear or change" (227). Although Hutch's work has changed from painting to poetry, the emphasis is still upon his eyes—and on his memory, to make visible whatever (like Rob) is *"out of sight"* (82).

The whole issue of the utility of art, and of what the artist gains or loses by his dedication, is raised again by Hutch's response to Vivien Leigh. A great actress, glimpsed at a moment when the public fails to recognize her, she becomes "a lucid emblem of his own destination or the long trip there: a life lived for others, though not at their request, ludicrously unneeded by them" (295). Rob had said the family at least would be grateful for Hutch's endeavor; Eborn, in *Love and Work*, discovered that his parents' ghosts were more interested in their love (however imperfect) than in any memorial images he might construct. Perhaps the artist is self-deluded in regarding himself as self-sacrificial; perhaps the outrider's messages are not vital to the group, or will not be acknowledged as such. These are questions that occur to Hutch and to his creator, but in fact there is little doubt that Hutch will persevere.

One aspect of the artist's concern with the past that comes through very strongly in the novel is the idea of place as somehow magnetic or radioactive. Hutch is "held as always by any revelation of the patience of objects (the willingness of grass and dirt and vines to sustain forever the energy of passionate gesture of speech . . .)" (290). That "willingness," of course, might instead be imputed to the artist-observer who solicits sensation; we may feel that Hutch's responses are melodramatic. But Price endorses this quality in Hutch and uses it in support of the surface-versus-center imagery which is as important to this novel as it was to *The Surface of Earth*. There are places that must be seen as entry-points, as manifestations of the spirit occurring upon the surface of earth and leading us toward the center of rest—toward what is called here "The Center of Gravity." The special quality of such places is that they have witnessed intense human desire, which can be satisfied (Price suggests) only by the "center"; their "patience" may be a result of God's willingness to help and redirect us, or may imply a still-potent usability for the artist.

Elaborate play is made with rocks, shards, and bricks discovered in these places; they remind us of that mineral kingdom in which a dreaming giant reigns, and of the whole cycle of human effort—building, falling into ruins, and the potential for building anew. The coin at Rachel's grave is an allied image; archeological remains may as well be recent as antique, for such differences (though awesome as layers of human experience) must pale in relation to eternity. Houses and rooms which have been important to Hutch's family are imbued with almost mystical significance; they appear frequently in dreams and are associated with the quest for perfect love (as dreamers move through houses), with cycles of ruin and repair. Also hallowed are American sites like Appomattox and Jamestown, Arthurian and other sites in Britain, Oxford, and Rome.

Eros

One of the most revealing of Hutch's responses to place occurs at Castle Gore, "surely one of the earth's main ganglia of love and its famished cry." He is fascinated by the possibility of incest, that Tristan (who loved Iseult, who was betrothed to King Mark) was Mark's son, rather than his nephew. Hutch has not felt the romantic imperative of which Iseult sings, and he explains that by Rachel's early death: "He thought that such a need must be taught, almost surely by a mother" (91). Tristan, accordingly, finds in Iseult the mother-goddess. As important for Price, however, in the erotic feeling that may occur between the generations is the father—suggested here by King Mark, and then by Tristan (who is linked by Hutch to Rob and chosen over Iseult, the female half of a primal pair). Hutch identifies himself, in the poem which he writes about Tristan and Iseult, with his narrator, " 'the gimp spare-leg, the wheyfaced witness' " (237). He both mocks and applauds his own destiny, in the light of Castle Gore's "great love and foul deceit" (92).

Erotic configurations in *The Source of Light* generally involve an incestuous attraction between the generations. A parallel is established, for instance, between mother and female lover by the dream in which Hutch says " '*Wait here*' " (126)—a request aimed at

Rachel and received by Ann. This is supported by a dream in which
Hutch sees the child in Ann's womb, since he claims to recall being
in Rachel's womb. Perhaps it is because Rachel did not stay that
Hutch is more frequently and intensely attracted to the young men
he associates with Rob. One very interesting dream has Ann and Lew
(a young Welshman soon to become Hutch's lover) in "the Garden"
with Hutch, enacting primeval male and female roles. Hutch wants
to make love with both mother Eve and father Adam and is "steadily
balked" (102). The ideal unit seems to be that of father, mother,
and child; the issue of wrong timing as an impediment to love is
implied when Rob, in his dream of *"Reward"* (197), imagines a
triangular meeting in which (as in the Garden dream) the principal
players are of approximately the same age.

The incestuous pattern is echoed by Grainger's nocturnal encounter
with Tossy, by Archie's approach to Hutch (a substitute for his dead
father), and by James's relationship to his daughter Nan. Typically,
an attractive "buccaneer" who is linked to Rob excites his child's
appetite for love. On one occasion Hutch dreams of being naked in
Rob's house, searching for him unsuccessfully, and having his anxiety
dissolve when he discovers James and Nan together in Rob's bed.
Behind Hutch's dream is the picture of "Rob and himself twenty
years ago, trailing through two states Rob's desperation and his own
plain contentment to be with a father who could make old rocks
in the road die laughing" (135). James also is traveling with his
child when Hutch meets them in a pub—a stolen child, in fact, so
that the Tommy Ryden plot of *A Generous Man* may be recalled.
Later, Hutch and James travel together by car, as Hutch does with
Rob at the beginning of the novel, clearly echoing that image with
which Price began his thinking about *Surface* and which he employed
also in "The Names and Faces of Heroes."

Most of the women in the novel, including the many walk-ons,
can be classified as needy, waiting types; most of the men are buccaneers. One especially striking case of this role definition occurs with
Archie's parents: the woman passing time in her cottage, the man
lost at sea. Price suggests an ancient history for such roles when Lew
in the Garden dream hunts rabbits while Ann sews their skins into
a quilt; or when Ann, referring to her lack of professional ambition,
says that she is *"a woman as old-style as anything painted on the walls
of caves"* (62); or when Alice suggests that Hutch should make the

fire—" 'Man's work. You burn, I cook' " (237). Such images connect with the artist as chilly, heroic outrider, roaming farther than ordinary males, and sending messages in to the "warmers," the primal pair by the fire.

Homosexual feeling is acknowledged directly for the first time in Price's fiction with *The Source of Light*. At least as an aspect of pan-sexuality, its presence will almost certainly have been felt before; Thorne Bradley, moreover, was seemingly in love with Forrest in *The Surface of Earth*. But now the protagonist has male lovers, and assorted other characters are given homosexual experiences or desires or awareness—all with very little fanfare or anxiety. We find a humorous reference to Oxford's " 'young hermits ... groveling on each other's butts before the plaster was dry on the walls' " (143), and another to a pair of Cambridge students " 'playing leapfrog for three nights straight' " (96). Rachel and Alice, we discover, were lovers; another woman, Joyce Meadows, refers in a veiled fashion to her desire for Rachel. Rob, very casually, writes to Hutch about a boyhood friend: *"he and I stayed steamed up about each other through that whole summer, all fumbling hands..."* (85). Both parents, then, supply a kind of precedent for Hutch—something genetic perhaps, or a suggestion of bisexuality as the human norm. (This surprising proliferation of homosexual references may be explained in part as a sign of changing times, a response to increasingly liberal attitudes toward homosexual relationships and their depiction in literature.)

Hutch has only two male lovers (Lew and Straw, his former student) as compared to two women (Ann and Marlene, a kindly prostitute); but other avatars of the desirable young male (Rowlet, Bailey, and James) seem to offset that careful balance, at least as indicators of a probable future. The icon of the beloved (either male or female) is an important motif in the novel, and Ann does achieve that status—in the Temple of the Magna Mater, for instance. Straw, however, or another male (by virtue of sharing Rob's gender) seems a more likely "mask of the thing Hutch hunted and worshiped in the world" (144). Straw is a "young god of Want and Use" (15) and an "inexhaustible ikon" (228); Lew also possesses an "Attic" (96), godlike beauty. Reminiscent perhaps of Wesley in *A Long and Happy Life*, these males have a more electric appeal, a stronger magnetism than any females in the book. Thus Lew has *"electric skin"* (284),

Straw is "no more kind or cruel than electric current" (15), and Bailey is made quasi-immortal as a lineman for the power company. Another sexual option, of course, is masturbation. A sane and reliable source of pleasure, it is also related to worship of the male god and to narcissism. The novel opens, in fact, with Hutch appreciatively regarding his penis in a mirror.

One of the novel's peculiarities is that it supplies abundant, vaguely Freudian data to "explain" Hutch's sexual interest in other men, and at the same time implicitly denies any need for explanation. We never see Hutch reflecting upon his homosexual liaisons, nor does he mention them to Ann. There are strong conflicting signals here, of perfect self-acceptance or deep repression. When he discusses with Alice the love that in Andrew Marvell's words is " 'begotten by despair / Upon impossibility' " (238), Hutch may be thinking of homosexuality—or, more probably, of the love that is experienced by solitaries. Similarly, when James appears in Hutch's rooms at Oxford, we do not really know what degree of sexual consciousness exists between them, or what will happen later. Our guesses may be naive or too labored, and there is more of this uncertainty than there needs to be: it obscures to some extent our vision of Hutch.

The one obvious, potential disadvantage of homosexual love is that it cannot involve the creation of a child. In a novel obsessed with generation and family trees this limitation does seem to matter. The plot device that moves us in that direction is abortion—of Straw's child, and then of Hutch's. Hutch thinks that Straw is "filthy past cleaning" (144), and Straw himself is tormented because of the first abortion: " 'I was hoping to really *make* something, the thing that matters' " (146). When Straw makes love to him, Hutch considers "asking one thing—'*Have you made something now?*' " (147). The abortion of Hutch's child (like Straw's) occurs without his complicity; and that may imply the hand of fate in making Hutch a solitary artist (who makes another thing that matters) or a homosexual. But he also causes Ann's choice by his lack of devotion, and profits from that choice because he feels released, and loses. An elaborate use of dolls (associated with Min and Grainger and Gracie and descending from old Rob's dolls, which Hutch takes to Oxford) suggests a continuing worship of generation (for these dolls are idols in a sense) and sadness at being "stopped" (46). Rabbit imagery extends this concern. Price draws upon the rabbit-pun lurking in Hutch's name.

the sexual and reproductive capacity of rabbits, and their status as
prey to create an emblem of dying generations.

Rob

Much of Rob's importance for Hutch is reflected in the poem he
writes after Rob's death. Recalling the mining imagery of *Surface*,
Rob is described as *"underground"* now and an " '*old mole in the
cellarage*' " (258); recalling also the incubus imagery, Hutch describes
himself as having been *"packed ... down—A dwarf in the mines"*
by the pressure that Rob brought to bear upon him, seeking *"bedrock"*
in a mere child. *"Press-ganged at birth"* (259) by Rob's charm,
Hutch still would not exchange his past for membership in the Cub
Scouts, a normal, peer-oriented boyhood. He describes himself and
Rob as *"circling a spot, mules at a mill. / The figure was rings, con-
centric rings / Round an unseen center (what were we grinding?) /
Till I fled and you quit"* (260). That image of futility, however,
gives way to a more positive version of the diagram or *"figure"* it is
Hutch's task to see, with his memory of the *"circular pool"* in which
he bathed with Rob at the novel's start. The water as a *"female essence"* brings Rachel into the charmed circle, permitting a triangular
embrace and leading Hutch to think of this moment as conception.
What began *"nine months ago"* at Warm Springs was Rob's death,
but that in fact is his *"best gift"* to Hutch. It releases Hutch for his
work and proves to him that it is possible to survive the loss of the
beloved. But it does more. At Warm Springs Rob had asked Hutch
to remember, and in the poem he does: as Hutch then had imitated
a drowning man, so Rob's "drowning" now of lung cancer is *"a mock-
death (mystery! a sleep / And a change)"* (261). Perfect love and
rest, an *"unseen center"* circled by mules, is found when the birth-
death cycle is complete.

Rob's dying is remarkably serene. He has learned to appreciate
solitude, has done what he could to honor his relationship with Min,
and has said (partly in a long, posthumous letter) all that he wants
to say to Hutch. His life feels complete to Rob, and he believes that
either rest or a *"more imaginative"* (215) future awaits him. The
vision that Rob experiences at the moment of death is both the central
passage of this novel and (especially given the long history of *Surface*)
perhaps the most intensely beautiful in all of Price's fiction. Rob finds
himself near "promised harbor"—a house we recognize as Hatt's, in

Bracey. He takes a lantern and moves through darkened rooms until
he finds another source of light (the novel's title comes partly from
this scene) and discovers there "his mother, himself, the room he is
born in. Feasible center, discovered in time, revised now and right."
The moment of death is also the moment of birth, and this time what
Rob has yearned for will be found. Images of birth and mock-death
and drowning converge as "the same dense wave that had drowned
his father" (210) raises Hutch—both father and son are safe. And
Rob's ghost, kindly visiting his sleeping son, is no longer needy.

Chapter Nine

The Integrity of a Single Vision

Reynolds Price is a writer whose strengths may be perceived as weaknesses, according to the disposition of the reader. The intensity of his language and vision will either compel readers or disengage them; there is not much room for a middle ground, except perhaps for recognition of the author's formidable intelligence. This is not to say that we must share the author's Christian faith or his belief in the difficulty of contingency in order to appreciate his work. We may view marriage, for instance, or the relationship of parents and child very differently from Price and still admire or even love the fiction. We must, however, grant the integrity and genuine passion of Reynolds Price if we are to penetrate the heart of his fiction and do him the justice of attention. He means every word he says; his manner leads to matter, not to the display of his linguistic facility. The surface of his work, however, has a stylized quality and a degree of polish that may tempt readers who are not in sympathy with his vision to suppose that Price's talents are restricted to the surface—that the author is hypnotized by the sound of his own voice.

In fact, there are few writers whose work suggests as strongly as Price's does the integrity of a single vision. The more deeply we penetrate into Price country the more insistent and thoroughly articulated does that vision appear. Nothing is accidental or extraneous or mere decoration. All of his elaborate imagery and the complex design of his fiction make final sense; each book repeats and expands the knowledge of the last. This intensity is ultimately a function of the author's concern with discovering the significance of his own life.

In *A Long and Happy Life* Price is apparently as remote from his own experience as he ever gets, and the success of that book (which many readers consider his best) complicates the picture of an artistic development that moves Price relentlessly always closer to the heart of his experience. That movement is unquestionably growth rather than a failure of the muse, and it is an exciting feature of his work for those readers who have followed it closely. *Love and Work* and

Permanent Errors, which take the author into his personal heart of darkness, are extraordinarily powerful and courageous works of fiction. In *The Surface of Earth* we find magnified into epic proportions the essence of all Price has learned in his previous delvings of the self's core; it is a book executed in perfect confidence, a kind of demonstration of the author's life earnings. Continuing that demonstration, *The Source of Light* returns to a sophisticated and contemporary scene, extending and confirming some of the artistic choices made with *Love and Work* and *Permanent Errors.* But still we are faced with what seems an anomaly—the suspicion that Price's first book may be his most valuable achievement. There is no accounting, finally, for the moment at which an author's finest work is cast up by his imagination. But if *A Long and Happy Life* is that book it should not lead us to the conclusion that Price's internal journey is a long mistake. Not all readers will feel inclined to follow him down those often-dark corridors of the self, but those who do will be amply compensated for their labor.

They will also be entertained, for Price knows how to tell a story. They will be amused, for he is often funny. And they will be instructed, for his vision is not so idiosyncratic that it cannot teach us much that is valuable for our own lives. The question of Price's stature relative to that of other twentieth-century American writers cannot yet be answered; too much depends upon the new directions that his work may take. He may discover that the monster as it has been defined so far, the secret embedded at the heart of all his work, has now very nearly been tracked down. Subsequent engagements may take him into unexpected country or still deeper recesses of essentially the same terrain. Certainly we may predict that in some guise his old themes will reappear. In any case, Reynolds Price has already produced enough valuable fiction to permit a safe guess that his name will endure.

Notes and References

Chapter One

1. Constance Rooke, "On Women and His Own Work: An Interview with Reynolds Price," *Southern Review* 14 (Autumn 1978):711.
2. Wallace Kaufman, "A Conversation with Reynolds Price," *Shenandoah* 17 (Spring 1966):22.
3. Reynolds Price, "Dodging Apples," in *Things Themselves; Essays and Scenes* (New York, 1972), p. 18.
4. Ibid., p. 19.
5. Reynolds Price, *Permanent Errors* (New York, 1970), p. 100.
6. Ibid., p. 101.
7. Eugene Moore, "An Interview with Reynolds Price on Writing, Readers, Critics," *Red Clay Reader* 3 (1966):24.
8. William Ray, *"Conversations: Reynolds Price & William Ray,"* *Bulletin of the Mississippi Valley Collection* 9 (Fall 1976):52.
9. Moore, "Writing, Readers, Critics," p. 21.
10. Ibid., p. 25 .
11. Kaufman, "A Conversation," pp. 24–25.
12. Reynolds Price, "Speaking of Books," *New York Times Book Review*, May 12, 1966, p. 13.
13. Kaufman, "A Conversation," p. 18.
14. Ibid., p. 13.
15. Price, "Speaking of Books . . . ," p. 12.
16. Kaufman, "A Conversation," p. 11.
17. Georges Gary, " 'A Great Deal More': Une Interview de Reynolds Price," *Recherches Anglaises et Americaines* 9 (1976):154.
18. Price, "News For the Mineshaft," in *Things Themselves*, p. 89.
19. Kaufman, "A Conversation," p. 9.
20. Price, "Dodging Apples," p. 6.
21. Price, "Speaking of Books," p. 2.
22. Price, "For Ernest Hemingway," in *Things Themselves*, p. 193.
23. Ibid., p. 198.
24. Ibid., p. 199.
25. Ibid., p. 181.
26. Ibid., p. 183.
27. Ibid., p. 179.
28. Ibid., p. 212.

29. Price, "The Onlooker, Smiling: An Early Reading of *The Optimist's Daughter,*" in *Things Themselves,* p. 124.

30. Ibid., p. 130.

31. Ibid., p. 134.

32. Price, "*The Wings of the Dove*: A Single Combat," in *Things Themselves,* p. 146.

33. Price, "*Pylon*: The Posture of Worship," in *Things Themselves,* p. 99.

34. Ibid., p. 100.

35. Price, "Speaking of Books," p. 2.

36. Price, "Dodo, Phoenix or Tough Old Cock," in *Things Themselves,* p. 170.

37. Gary, "'A Great Deal More,'" p. 145.

38. Louis D. Rubin, Jr., *The Writer in the South: Studies in a Literary Community,* (Athens: University of Georgia Press, 1972), p. 33.

39. Kaufman, "A Conversation," p. 19.

40. Ibid., p. 18.

41. Price, "Dodo, Phoenix or Tough Old Cock," in *Things Themselves,* p. 168.

42. Ibid., p. 174.

43. Kaufman, "A Conversation," p. 6.

44. Reynolds Price, *A Palpable God* (New York, 1978), p. 10.

45. Ibid., p. 41.

46. Rooke, "On Women and His Own Work," p. 709.

47. Ibid., p. 708.

48. Ray, "Conversations," p. 32.

49. Gary, "'A Great Deal More,'" p. 148.

50. Rooke, "On Women and His Own Work," p. 719.

51. Price, *A Palpable God,* p. 60.

52. Kaufman, "A Conversation," p. 12.

Chapter Two

1. Kaufman, "A Conversation," p. 18.

2. Reynolds Price, "*A Long and Happy Life*: Fragments of Groundwork," *Virginia Quarterly Review* 41 (Spring 1965):240.

3. Reynolds Price, *A Long and Happy Life* (New York, 1962), p. 66; hereafter page references cited in the text.

4. Price, "Fragments of Groundwork," p. 241.

5. Rooke, "On Women and His Own Work," p. 723.

6. Ibid., p. 175.

7. Price, "Fragments of Groundwork," p. 247.

8. Rooke, "On Women and His Own Work," p. 724.

9. Moore, "Writing, Readers, Critics," p. 26.

10. Reynolds Price, *Early Dark* (New York, 1977), p. vii; hereafter page references cited in the text.

Chapter Three

1. Reynolds Price, *The Names and Faces of Heroes* (New York, 1963), p. 3; hereafter page references cited in the text.

2. Price, "Fragments of Groundwork," p. 242.

3. Reynolds Price, "A Story and Why," *Duke Alumni Register*, April, 1963, p. 33.

4. Price, "Dodging Apples," in *Things Themselves*, p. 14.

5. Ibid., p. 19.

6. Ibid., p. 20.

7. Kaufman, "A Conversation," p. 18.

Chapter Four

1. Price, "News for the Mineshaft" in *Things Themselves*; hereafter cited in text as *NM* followed by page number.

2. Reynolds Price, *A Generous Man* (New York, 1966), p. 275; hereafter page references cited in the text.

3. Quoted in "News for the Mineshaft," p. 84.

4. Dante Alighieri, *Purgatory*, trans. Dorothy L. Sayers (New York: Basic Books, 1962), canto 30, lines 73–75.

Chapter Five

1. Reynolds Price, *Love and Work* (New York, 1968) p. 19; hereafter page references cited in the text.

2. Moore, "Writing, Readers, Critics," p. 22.

3. John Wain, "Puppeteers," *New York Review of Books*, August 23, 1968, p. 35.

4. Geoffrey Wolff, "Murder Your Darlings," *New Leader*, June 17, 1968, p. 24.

5. Daniel Frederick Daniel, "Within and Without a Region: The Fiction of Reynolds Price," Ph.D. diss., University of Wisconsin–Madison, 1977, pp. 97–98.

6. Rooke, "On Women and His Own Work," p. 707.

Chapter Six

1. Reynolds Price, *Permanent Errors* (New York, 1970), p. vii; hereafter page references cited in the text.

2. Price, *Love and Work*, p. 74.

3. Ibid., p. 58.

Chapter Seven

1. Richard Gilman, "A mastodon of a novel, by Reynolds Price: *The Surface of Earth*," *New York Times Book Review*, June 29, 1975, p. 4.

2. Eudora Welty responded to Gilman's review in a letter to the editor of the *New York Times Book Review* July 20, 1975, pp. 24–25.

3. Kaufman, "A Conversation," p. 12.

4. Reynolds Price, *The Surface of Earth* (New York, 1975), p. 6; hereafter page references cited in the text.

5. Reynolds Price, *Presence and Absence: Versions from the Bible* (Columbia, 1974), p. 41.

6. Romans 8:18.

Chapter Eight

1. Reynolds Price, *The Source of Light* (New York, 1981), p. 55; hereafter page references cited in the text.

Selected Bibliography

PRIMARY SOURCES

1. Novels

A Generous Man. New York: Atheneum, 1966. London: Chatto & Windus, 1967. Reprints: New York: Signet, 1967; Avon, 1973.

A Long and Happy Life. New York: Atheneum, 1962. London: Chatto & Windus, 1962. Reprints: New York: Avon, 1963, 1969. London: Penguin, 1964.

Love and Work. New York: Atheneum, 1968. London: Chatto & Windus, 1968. New York: Atheneum, 1975 (reprint).

The Source of Light. New York: Atheneum, 1981.

The Surface of Earth. New York: Atheneum, 1975. New York: Avon, 1976 (reprint). London: Arlington, 1977.

2. Short Story Collections

The Names and Faces of Heroes. New York: Atheneum, 1963. London: Chatto & Windus, 1963. Reprints: New York: Avon, 1966; Atheneum, 1973.

Permanent Errors. New York: Atheneum, 1970. London: Chatto & Windus, 1971.

3. Play

Early Dark: A Play. New York: Atheneum, 1977.

4. Poetry

The Annual Heron. New York: Albondocani, 1980.

A Final Letter. Los Angeles: Sylvester & Orphanos, 1980.

Late Warning: Four Poems. New York: Albondocani, 1968.

Lessons Learned: Seven Poems. New York: Albondocani, 1977.

5. Essays and Translations

Nine Mysteries (Four Joyful, Four Sorrowful, One Glorious). Winston Salem: Palaemon Press, 1979.

Oracles: Six Versions from the Bible. Durham: The Friends of Duke University, 1977.

A Palpable God: Thirty Stories Translated from the Bible with an Essay on the Origins and Life of Narrative. New York: Atheneum, 1978.
Presence and Absence: Versions from the Bible. Columbia: Bruccoli and Clark, 1974.
Things Themselves: Essays and Scenes. New York: Atheneum, 1972.

6. Individual Poems
"The Annual Heron." *Poetry* (December, 1979), pp. 154–60.
"At the Gulf." *American Review* 17 (May, 1973):148–50.
"Damon's Epitaph" in *Symbolism and Modern Literature: Studies in Honor of Wallace Fowlie.* Durham: Duke University Press, 1978, pp. 165–70.
"The Dream of a House." Winston-Salem: Palaemon Press. December 1977.
"The Dream of Lee." *Massachusetts Review* 20 (Autumn 1979):468–71.
"Five Versions." *Archive* 83 (Autumn 1970):40–42.
"Genesis 15, Deuteronomy 32." *St. Andrews Review* 2 (Fall and Winter 1973):210.
["I say of any man..."] "After Hölderlin." *Encounter* 17 (November, 1961):4.
"The Lines of Life." *Shenandoah* 17 (Winter 1966):69.
"Man and Faun." *The Carolina Quarterly* 21 (Spring 1969):17–19.
"Naked Boy." *The Carolina Quarterly* 31 (Winter 1978):13–16.
"Pure Boys and Girls" in *For Aaron Copland.* Winston-Salem: Palaemon Press, 1978.
"Seven Poems about Death." *Shenandoah* 23 (Summer 1972):74–75.
"Socrates and Alcibiades" in *For Robert Penn Warren.* Winston-Salem: Palaemon Press, 1980.
"Three Versions of Two Poems by Michelangelo." *Archive* 88 (Spring 1976):12–13.
"To My Niece: Our Photograph, in a Hammock." *Southern Review* 8 (Autumn 1972):912–14.
"Torso of an Archai Apollo." New York: Albondocani Press. December 1969.
"Two Versions from the Bible." *Shenandoah* 21 (Spring 1970):150–51.

7. Uncollected Articles
"Family Stories: The Carters in Plains." *Time,* January 3, 1977, pp. 26, 29.
"Given Time: Beginning *The Surface of Earth.*" *Antaeus* 21, no. 2 (Spring–Summer 1976):57–64.
"God Bless the Child Who Reads." *Esquire,* March, 1976, pp. 94, 129–30.
"Home: An American Obsession." *Saturday Review* November 26, 1977, pp. 9–16.

"*A Long and Happy Life*: Fragments of Groundwork." *Virginia Quarterly Review* 41 (Spring 1965):236–47.
"A Question of Influence." *New York Times Book Review*, May 29, 1966, pp. 2, 12, 13.
"The South: A Proud Moment." *Washington Post* [Special Inaugural Section], January 20, 1977, pp. 1, 14, 15.
"A Story and Why." *Duke Alumni Register* 49, no. 4 (April, 1963): 31–33.
"Two Years Underway: Pages from a Notebook." *Archive* 89 (Spring 1977):7–17.
"What Did Emma Bovary Do In Bed?" *Esquire*, August, 1973, pp. 80, 144, 146.

SECONDARY SOURCES

1. Critical Essays
Barnes, Daniel. "The Names and Faces of Reynolds Price." *Kentucky Review* 2 ii (1968):76–91. A useful study of Price's early works with emphasis on the significance of faces and names.
Eichelberger, Clayton L. "Reynolds Price: 'A Banner in Defeat.'" *Journal of Popular Culture* 1 (1967):410–17. Balances earlier views of Price's first works which proposed mainly optimistic readings.
Freeman, Anne Hobson. "Penetrating a Small Patch of *The Surface of Earth*." *Virginia Quarterly Review* 51 (Autumn 1975):637–41. A positive, general look at Price's Southern epic.
Shepherd, Allen. "Love (and Marriage) in *A Long and Happy Life*." *Twentieth Century Literature* 17 (January, 1971):20–35. A close and careful look at the comic potential of Price's first novel.
———. "*Love and Work* and the Unseen World." *Topic* 23 (Spring 1972):52–57. A study of the supernatural elements of the novel.
———. "Notes on Nature in the Fiction of Reynolds Price." *Critique: Studies in Modern Fiction* 2 (1970):83–94. A study of the ways in which nature both informs and reflects the action in Price's works through *Permanent Errors*.
Stevenson, John W. "The Faces of Reynolds Price's Short Fiction." *Studies in Short Fiction* 3 (1966):300–306. A look at Price's first short story collection as studies in the obligations of love.
Vauthier, Simone. "The 'Circle in the Forest': Fictional Space in Reynolds Price's *A Long and Happy Life*." *Mississippi Quarterly* 28 (Spring 1975):123–46. A highly intelligent, detailed study of the relation between psychological and geographical territories.
———. "Nom et Visage dans *A Long and Happy Life*." *Recherches*

Anglaises et Americaines 5 (1971):243–63. A careful and sophisticated study of the quest for identity in *A Long and Happy Life.*

2. Sample Reviews

A Generous Man
Hicks, Granville. "In Pursuit of a Snake Named Death." *Saturday Review,* March 26, 1966, pp. 27–28.
Wain, John. "Mantle of Faulkner." *The New Republic,* May 14, 1966, pp. 31–33. A negative review which seeks to brand Price as an imitator of Faulkner.

A Long and Happy Life
Hicks, Granville. "Country Girl Burdened with Love." *Saturday Review,* March 10, 1962, pp. 17–18. One example of the enthusiastic response to Price's first novel.

Love and Work
Wain, John. "Puppeteers." *New York Review of Books,* August 22, 1968, p. 35. Representative of the mixed reaction to this novel.
Wolff, Geoffrey. " 'Murder Your Darling.' " *New Leader,* June 17, 1968, pp. 24–25. A negative review arguing the author's self-indulgence.

The Names and Faces of Heroes
Gilman, Richard. "This Is the Way It Happened." *New York Times Book Review,* June 30, 1963, p. 4. Negative only because of its elaborately qualified praise.

Permanent Errors
Davenport, Guy. "Doomed, damned and unaware: *Permanent Errors." New York Times Book Review,* October 11, 1970, p. 4.
Solotaroff, Theodore. "The Reynolds Price Who Outgrew Southern Pastoral." *Saturday Review,* September 26, 1970, pp. 27, 28, 29, 46. A concerted, positive effort to place the collection in the overall progression of Price's work.

The Source of Light
Oates, Joyce Carol. "Portrait of the Artist as Son, Lover, Elegist." *New York Times Book Review,* April 26, 1981, pp. 3, 30.
Woiwode, Larry. "Pursuits of the Flesh, Adventures of the Spirit." *Washington Post Book World,* April 26, 1981, p. 5.

The Surface of Earth
Gilman, Richard. "A mastodon of a novel, by Reynolds Price." *New York Times Book Review,* June 29, 1975, p. 4. An influential negative review which nevertheless acknowledges the book's power.

Gurganus, Allan. *Washington Post Book World*, July 13, 1975, pp. 1, 14, 15. A favorable review which explores the book's biblical and epic characteristics.

3. Interviews

Gary, Georges. "'A Great Deal More': Une Interview de Reynolds Price." *Recherches Anglaises et Americaines* 9 (1976):135–54.

Kaufman, Wallace. "A Conversation with Reynolds Price." *Shenandoah* 17 (Summer 1966):3–25. Expanded in "Notice, I'm Still Smiling," in *Kite Flying and Other Irrational Acts*. Edited by John Carr. Baton Rouge: Louisiana State University, 1972, pp. 70–95.

Moore, Eugene. "An Interview with Reynolds Price on Writing, Readers, Critics." *Red Clay Reader* 3 (1966):18–26.

Ray, William. "*Conversations: Reynolds Price & William Ray.*" *Bulletin of the Mississippi Valley Collection* 9 (Fall 1976):8–82.

Rooke, Constance. "On Women and His Own Work: An Interview with Reynolds Price." *Southern Review* 14 (Autumn 1978):706–25.

4. Dissertation

Daniel, Daniel Frederick. "Within and Without a Region: The Fiction of Reynolds Price." Ph.D. dissertation, University of Wisconsin-Madison, 1977.

Index

56-60; question of its genre, 57-58; Rooster Pomeroy (character), 64-71 passim; Rosacoke (character), 60-63; sexuality in, 60-63, 64, 66, 67; supernatural in, 57, 67, 68-71; Tom (character), 66-68

Long and Happy Life, A, 3, 6, 7, 10, *15-39,* 40, 43, 47, 48, 112, 144, 145; animals, images of, 26-27, 31; babies, reproduction as theme, 18-19, 20, 21, 22, 27, 30, 35-36; blacks in, 18-19; Christianity in, 32, 34-36; "circular space," nature in, 16-19, 21; Isaac Alston (character), 27-28; love/solitude dichotomy in, 28-29, 30-31, 33, 38-39; Milo (character), 29; plot summary, 15-16; Rosacoke (character), 20-22, 23, 24, 26, 29, 30-33, 38-39; sexuality in, 19, 21-28, 32; style, 36-38; temptation-sin-redemption pattern, 15-16; Wesley (character), 18, 20, 21, 22-27, 28, 29, 31, 32, 33, 38-39

Love and Work, 3, 7, *75-86,* 87, 144-45; as autobiography, 75; critics' reactions to, 75, 76; Eborn (character), 77-80, 81-85 passim; Eborn's novel, 83-84; Eborn's work essay, 80-82; image of "incest and matricide," 82-83; imagery in, 78-80; Jane (character), 83-85; literary allusions in, 77, 78; Lou (character), 82-83; plot summary, 75-77; sexuality in, 85; supernaturalism in, 85-86

Source of Light, The, 3, *134-43,*

145; blacks in, 134; erotic elements in, 138-42; homosexuality in, 140-41; Hutch's "life plan," 135-38; idea of "place" in, 137-38; imagery of building-ruins-rebuilding, 138; love/solitude dichotomy in, 136; plot summary, 134-35; Rob (character), 142-43; as sequel to *Surface of Earth,* 134; solitary artist theme, 136-37

Surface of the Earth, The, 3, 56, *111-33,* 134, 140, 145; blacks in, 130-32; Book One, "Absolute Pleasures," 112-16; Book Two, "The Heart in Dreams," 116-21; Book Three, "Partial Amends," 121-26; Christianity, bibilical allusions in, 132-33; controversy about, 111; dreams in, 129-30; genesis of, 112; imagery in, 126-29; love/solitude dichotomy in, 112, 113, 117, 120, 121, 124; reviewers' reactions to, 111; searching as central metaphor, 112; sexuality in, 113, 114, 115, 117, 122, 127-28

WORKS: PLAYS
Early Dark, 3, 38-39
Long and Happy Life, A, 3

WORKS: POETRY
"Annual Heron, The," 10

WORKS: SHORT STORIES
Names and Faces of Heroes, The, 2, 3, *40-55:*
"Anniversary, The," 46-48
"Chain of Love, A," 40-42